To (
Hope you enjo(
story. Than(
being his frien(
Love, Diane Coles

Still Smiling

The Life Story of Bradley Taylor Coles

by Diane Taylor Coles

Still Smiling

The Life Story of
Bradley Taylor Coles

Authors Note: The names of the doctors have been changed to protect their privacy. We greatly appreciate their skilled medical treatment that gave Brad so many years of quality life. The staff at Stanford Children's Hospital, and especially at Primary Children's Hospital, became an extension of our family.

For information regarding copies of this book, please contact:
Diane Taylor Coles at dcoles6@csi.com
Or purchase a copy on our website:
www.adrac.com

Designed by David B. Coles

Printed in the United States of America

PREFACE

After reading a book entitled *I'd Rather Be Writing*, I came to the conclusion that I would actually rather be reading, or perhaps shopping. Writing is hard work, as anyone who has attempted to turn thoughts into printed text can affirm. However, I am required to write this story. Bradley gave me that assignment before he died, though I only found out later. As I was looking through the last journal that he kept before his death, I turned to the back cover, and there it was, written up at the top: "If possible, please try to make my life history into a story that all people can read when I am dead." Well, as stated in *The Cat in the Hat Comes Back*, "he picked out (a somebody),---me," to write that story for him. Who else did he think would find his journal and read that sentence?

The journal that he kept was filled with his personality, with experiences expressed as only he could tell them and words spelled as only he could spell (or not spell). I am including some of Brad's writings in this story to make it more personal. Ultimately though, this is my story, my memories as I recall them. A teacher in one of my writing classes stated, "Memory is truth." As well as I remember, the experiences told here are true. They are my memories of a special son, who enriched my life and the lives of all around him.

One night not long ago as I was preparing for bed, a picture came into my mind, a visual image of the experiences of our family. I pictured us on the crest of a wave in the ocean, on the top of the world with a spectacular view. We sailed smoothly along, enjoying ourselves immensely. But the moment didn't last. The next thing I knew we were crashing onto the shore, thrown down hard, like so much seaweed. The wave receded, going farther and farther from view, leaving behind a huge expanse of wet sand. Would the wave ever return? Would we have the chance to be on top again? It was so unfair. We had worked hard to get to the top, only to be thrown unceremoniously to the ground. The receding wave seemed to represent years of progress that were lost.

But then another thought occurred to me. When the tide is out, we have an opportunity to look for treasures in the sand. Throughout Brad's life, each setback left us sitting in the wet sand. Each also exposed to us treasures that we would have found in no other way. I have tried to look at the memories in light of those treasures. Do I wish Brad's life had been long and healthy? Of course I do. But I have tried to save up the treasures he left us, his legacy, to pass on to others as he wished me to do. His is a life worth remembering.

PROLOGUE

Shane and I got off the elevator on the main floor of the hospital and walked toward the exit. I explained again to my nine-year-old son how sick his brother Brad was and that the doctors probably would not be able to make him well this time. I was afraid our quota of miracles had run out, and Bradley would probably die soon.

"I know," said Shane. "You already told me." We zipped our coats against the late December night air as we walked through the exit doors.

"Mom, why doesn't someone come up with a cure for cancer?" Shane asked me. Very good question, I thought. I explained that scientists and doctors had been trying for many years to find a cure, treatments were helping people to live longer, and some people were considered cured. But the disease was still not preventable and existing treatments did not work every time.

I suggested, "Maybe when you grow up, Shane, you'll be the one to find a cure for cancer."

He thought for a moment and said, "Well, even if I did, wouldn't it be too late to help Brad?"

I sighed and felt the weight of his words. "Yes, Shane, it would be too late for Brad."

Coles family on vacation in Maui, Hawaii, Summer 1992 (From left to right: Dave, Shane, Nathan, Diane, Kristi, Bradley, Janene, Alisa)

Chapter 1

EASTER BABY, 1982

I glanced at my watch as I turned the dress to sew the next section of hem. I usually liked making matching Easter dresses for my three little girls, but this year time had gotten away from me, and I was racing the clock to have them done for church the following morning. Two dresses were completely finished and the third was well under way. That was in addition to the little suit I had sewn for Nathan consisting of pants, a matching vest, and a white shirt. It was a lot of trouble for a two year old, but he would look so cute dressed up for Easter Sunday with his sisters, who would have their new dresses. However, I was getting the distinct impression I would not be seeing them in their new outfits on Easter morning. It was already about 8:00 p.m., and I was going into labor. There were no steady contractions yet, but since this was my fifth pregnancy, I had a pretty good idea that things were starting to happen.

I had gone for my weekly checkup just the day before. My doctor had assured me it would be several more days until the baby would be born and that I should make an appointment for the following week. Now as I sewed, I thought about all those Easter eggs we had colored. I knew our children were looking forward to finding them in our traditional egg hunt. I tried to ignore my uneasy feelings and finish the project at hand.

Near midnight I crawled into bed, deciding that if I could sleep I was not really in labor. The Easter outfits were finished and set out with their respective socks and shoes. I dozed on and off for a few hours, envying my husband Dave's steady snoring. Finally, in the early morning hours, I accepted the fact that I would not be spending Easter morning in church. I delayed waking Dave as long as I dared. About 6:00 a.m. we dropped off our sleepy children with their new clothes and Easter baskets at our friends' home and headed to the hospital.

I was very familiar with San Jose's Good Samaritan Hospital. Only twenty-three months before I had given birth there to Nathan and twenty-two months before that to Janene. Our oldest daughter, Alisa, had been born in Provo, Utah, during our student days. Kristi, our second child, had been born in the Kaiser Hospital in Santa Clara, California. With the birth of every child I have had the same impression on the way to the hospital: "I don't want to do this right now." But this time, I was comforted by the thought that I was going to receive medication to block the pain. The thought of a fifth natural birth did not appeal to me, and a pain-free delivery was in my plan.

Things did not go exactly as I had anticipated. When I was admitted, my doctor was still in bed (lucky guy), and the doctor on call did not want to authorize an epidural. During our discussion he actually said, "You have given birth four times without medication. I'm sure you could do it again." I wonder how many times he had given birth without medication. He obviously missed the point entirely.

"Yes," I told him. "I have had four children completely naturally, which is exactly why I am requesting the epidural."

We had been at the hospital about three hours by the time my doctor arrived. He kindly agreed to the epidural and made the necessary arrangements. I was especially grateful to be getting the pain medication since my doctor had determined that the baby was in a posterior position, which was contributing to slow progress in the labor. I had never been in labor more than eight hours, but he seemed to think this time could be different. Dave and I tried to keep ourselves occupied, but there wasn't much to do in those pre-birthing-room days except stare at the wallpaper and time the contractions.

By the time the pain medication and an anesthesiologist finally arrived I had been at the hospital over four hours. The progress of all that sustained labor was depressingly slow. In order to put the epidural needle into my spinal column the doctor had me turn over. It sounds easy enough, but while having contractions every two minutes, I found it a painful ordeal. I was very uncomfortable and not especially thrilled with the doctor, but I cooperated as much as possible, anticipating the pleasure of numbness.

After I returned to a more normal position things started to progress very quickly. Apparently when I had turned over the baby had turned also and was anxious to make an entrance into the world. In a matter of minutes I was being wheeled into the delivery room

Since things happened so quickly, the epidural had not had time to take effect. All my hopes for a pain-free delivery were not realized. At 11:52 a.m. we welcomed our new son into the world. We hadn't known ahead of time whether we would have a boy or a girl, since it was not common then to do ultrasounds. We were thrilled to have another boy. Nathan had been considerably outnumbered by sisters, and a little brother would even things up a bit. Bradley Taylor Coles weighed in at seven pounds, two ounces and was nineteen-and-a-half inches long. He was a beautiful baby. Soon after his birth the epidural medication took effect. The bottom half of my body went thoroughly numb and stayed that way for several hours.

The date was April 11, 1982. It was an amazing coincidence that Bradley had been born on the same date as his Grandma Taylor and that his Grandma Coles had also been born on an Easter Sunday, though on a different date. Or maybe it was not a coincidence. There were so many miracles in Brad's life, it is not hard to believe that his birth date was part of a heavenly plan to remind us how special he was. We chose his middle name, Taylor, because it is my maiden name, but his first name is just one we liked. Dave was teased by his fellow employees at FMC Corporation that he had named his son after the Bradley Fighting Vehicle, an armored personnel carrier for the Army, which Dave's division of the company was working on at that time. Perhaps naming him after an armored vehicle would have been appropriate. He proved to be almost invincible.

Chapter 2

WINDOW TO THE SOUL

We brought Brad home when he was three days old, and he became Nathan's roommate. A few weeks later on the first Sunday in May, we took Brad to church where he was given a name and a father's blessing. His Grandpa Taylor was there to participate in the ordinance. Dave almost named him Nathan and had to correct himself before coming up with the right name. I made a note in Brad's baby book that he was blessed to be obedient to his parents and that he would help prepare for the Second Coming of the Savior. I was a little perturbed that Dave had said nothing about him serving a church mission or being married in an LDS temple. I thought maybe he had been so distracted by almost giving both his sons the same name that he had forgotten to finish the whole blessing. However, when I discussed the blessing with Dave later, he told me that he felt impressed to not give the usual father's blessing, though he did not know why at the time.

After Bradley's birth, we were ready for a break from having children. Five children in just under seven years was my limit. Even though it was a challenge to keep up with all those little people, most of the time I thoroughly enjoyed our large family.

Alisa and Kristi learned early how to take responsibility. Alisa was serious, and used vocabulary far in advance of her age. At school recess, she could often be found walking around with the playground aides, known as "Yard Duties," rather than playing with her classmates. Kristi was a born organizer who loved to vacuum the carpets and clean her dresser drawers. Janene's greatest goal in life was to have fun, and Nathan was a peacemaker. Bradley soon began to compete with Janene for the title of family clown. He learned to roll his eyes back in his head and make a goofy face. We couldn't help laughing at him even when he was in trouble, which was a frequent event.

By the time he was eighteen months old, Bradley could unlock the front door and escape. Dave installed a lock at the very top of the door to keep him inside. One morning I walked the girls out to our friend's car for a ride to school. Nathan followed me and Brad stayed behind. I heard the sound of the dead bolt lock turning and realized that Brad had locked us out. Fortunately, we had a spare key hidden in the backyard shed, so Nathan and I were able to get back into the house.

Bradley was amazingly fast at making messes. One day he dumped out an entire bottle of soy sauce, and while I was cleaning that up, he pulled all the books off the bottom bookshelf, removed their covers, crumpled them up, and threw them in the garbage. That same day he threw away the bib he had been wearing. Another time Bradley found an old soda can at the neighbors' and, after sampling the contents, ended up with a mouthful of ants. In case anyone wants to know how ants taste, he said they were yucky.

When I was hurrying to finish errands one afternoon, I broke one of my own rules. I left all five kids in the van while I ran into the office at the school for a few minutes. Later that night when I was giving Bradley a bath, I noticed a round red spot on his cheek with kind of a bulls-eye in the center. I had no idea what it was, and none of the other kids offered any information. I decided he must have bumped his face on something. The next morning when I got into the van, I noticed the cigarette lighter on the floor. Strange, we don't smoke. Then suddenly it made sense. Brad's previously unidentified red mark now had a source. He wasn't badly burned, but the mark remained faintly visible the rest of his life. I never did understand how he managed to heat up the lighter and brand himself, but I had discovered another good reason for not leaving the kids unattended in the car.

Bradley became a daddy's boy. He would ask me dozens of times a day if Daddy would be home for dinner. Since Dave traveled frequently for business, he was usually gone several days each month. When he was in town, as soon as he came in the door after work, Brad would tackle his legs and not let him out of his sight the rest of the evening. He liked to use tools like Dad and was happy for hours in the garage with a hammer, pounding on an old piece of metal.

Bradley learned to talk on schedule, but he was more interested in action than conversation. When we took family walks we stopped bringing a stroller for him, since he preferred to get out and run.

Although Bradley was happy, active, and appeared healthy, sometimes Dave would say something to me about Brad not looking well. I always dismissed his concerns, but I too had the feeling that something was not right. He grew very slowly, staying on the lowest percentile of the doctor's growth charts. But that was not the source of my worry. It was in his eyes, in his case, literally the window to his soul. When I looked at him I would feel unsettled, like a premonition of troubling things to come.

One Saturday morning I was lying in bed enjoying the quiet that would not last and gathering my strength for the day ahead. Opening my eyes, I saw standing in the doorway of my bedroom the tiny figure of two-year-old Bradley, dressed in his yellow blanket sleeper. He had climbed out of his crib and was waiting to see my reaction to his escape. As he flashed me one of his irresistible smiles, I had the thought come to my mind, "Remember this; this is a gift." He ran over and jumped up into bed with me. I snuggled him next to me and wondered, "What is in store for this tiny, special child?"

Two-year-old Brad before his diagnosis, playing at Jenney Lake, Wyoming, 1984

Chapter 3

A NEW PERSPECTIVE

Each day of the week we had a set schedule of lessons and activities. All three girls were involved in dance lessons, gymnastics, Girl Scouts, or piano lessons. During the mornings Nathan attended a co-op preschool, which I taught two days a month. I used the hours he was gone to grocery shop and do other errands. I could accomplish those tasks much faster with only Bradley. He became my little buddy during the times we spent together. He actually loved to shop, which was a wonderful surprise. Both Dave and Nathan felt that shopping was torture, so I had assumed that was a genetic trait for the males in our family. When he was at home Brad never held still, but he sat patiently in a shopping cart or stroller and enjoyed being out among other people.

The third week of February 1985 was full of the usual activities and lessons. Dave was out of town on one of his frequent business trips, which meant that there was no relief for me at the end of the day. On Tuesday I had dropped him off at the airport to catch a flight to Dallas, Texas. There he had rented a car for a three-hour drive to the town of Kileen, his destination. He would return Friday afternoon, in time to spend the weekend on a family outing.

We were planning a weekend trip to play in the snow in the Sierras. My parents lived near Sacramento, so we would stay with them Friday night and drive to the mountains the following day. The kids looked forward to this adventure every year, since it was their only chance to see snow. It was also fun for them to stay with their grandparents.

On Tuesday when Dave left, Brad had sounded a little congested. That night he became much worse, and coughed all night. I was not surprised. Someone seemed to get sick whenever Dave was out of town. I could have put it on my calendar. Brad's cough came from deep in his chest, like when he had gotten bronchitis once before. First thing in the morning I called our pediatrician's office for an appointment for Bradley. I wanted him to be well enough by the weekend to have fun on our trip.

That afternoon I already had appointments, scheduled months in advance, for the four older children to have their teeth examined by our pediatric dentist. His office was not far from the pediatrician's, so I arranged to drop off the other kids there and then take Brad to the doctor during their appointment.

Everything was going according to plan. I left the four older kids in the supervised play area at the dentist's office. Brad and I made the short drive to Dr. Green's office. He saw us right away and confirmed my suspicion about bronchitis. After writing a prescription for antibiotics, the doctor started to leave the room. With his hand on the doorknob, he paused and asked if there was anything else concerning me. I told him that I thought Bradley looked a little pale, which could have been explained by the bronchitis. He agreed and suggested a blood test to see if his iron level was low.

The nurse came and did a quick finger prick for the blood sample. When she examined the slide she became concerned and asked the doctor for advice. The iron level was dangerously low, and there was something else that troubled him. He asked me to go next door to the lab so they could draw a larger blood sample and do a more thorough test.

My anxiety level suddenly increased. I was nervous about Bradley, but I also needed to pick up the other children at the dentist's office. I told Dr. Green that I didn't have time to visit the lab, and especially not to wait for results from the test, as he had requested. He insisted that the test needed to be done right away. He called the lab to tell them I was coming, and I rushed Brad over. As soon as the blood was drawn, I hurried to retrieve the other children. They were all finished with their exams, and I distractedly paid the bill and scheduled follow-up appointments. Rounding up jackets and new toothbrushes, I herded them all into the van.

It was late afternoon as we returned to the doctor's office for the lab test results. Dr. Green had told me the lab would call his office when the tests were done. When the lab technician came in person to talk with him, I could tell something awful was in store, but I had no idea what might be wrong.

After meeting privately with the doctor, the technician left, glancing in my direction. The receptionist, with a serious, stricken expression, called me back to the doctor's office, telling me she would keep an eye on the kids in the waiting room. We were the only ones remaining in the office by that time. When I saw the pained expression on the face of the nurse and then the doctor, my breath caught in my throat. Over the years, I would see that look many more times, a sure sign that bad news was coming.

Dr. Green explained there were several abnormalities in the blood and Bradley would require some sort of hospital treatment. He wouldn't give me any more details, saying he would need to talk with a hematologist about the best course of action and would call me first thing in the morning.

On the half-hour drive home, I had to concentrate to keep my mind on San Jose's rush-hour traffic. The children, tired and hungry, were getting cranky. What should I say to prepare them for an illness that was as yet unidentified? I was tense, aching inside, and wishing desperately that Dave was in town. The kids could tell I was upset. I told them I was worried about Bradley because he might be very sick. They instantly became concerned about their baby brother and sat quietly the rest of the way home.

The phone rang moments after we walked in the door. When I answered and heard Dr. Green's voice, I thought, "He's not supposed to call until morning." I didn't want to think of the implications of his call coming sooner.

"I just talked to the hematologist," he explained. "He wants you to take Bradley to Stanford Children's Hospital tonight, as soon as you can get there. They are expecting you." He still wouldn't tell me what was wrong, not wanting me to worry needlessly until an accurate diagnosis was made. When I pressed him for information he relented.

"It could be leukemia."

I leaned against the kitchen counter for support and gasped for breath. Alisa and Kristi stared at me as I put my hand over my face and tried to make sense of what I had just heard.

The doctor continued, "Leukemia is no longer a death sentence. If that is what Bradley has, there is a good chance that after treatment he will be cured. In certain types of leukemia the cure rate is about 70 percent." I know I was supposed to feel reassured by that news, but I could only think that my baby might die, Dave wasn't in town, and I had four other small children who still needed to eat dinner; I didn't even know where Stanford Medical Center was. I needed help.

I told the girls Brad might have cancer, since they had never heard of leukemia, and that I needed to make some phone calls. I went into the bedroom, shut the door, and dialed Dave's hotel room in Texas. Thank goodness he was there. There was no easy way to convey the information I needed to tell him. I could almost hear the color drain from his face as I told him

Brad's life might be in danger. His voice was unsteady as he assured me he would be on the first possible flight home.

With a three-hour drive back to Dallas and then having to wait for the next available flight, Dave would not be back until sometime the next day. I next called my parents in Sacramento. My mom, who was an elementary school teacher, said she would get a substitute for the rest of the week and come immediately. It would take her more than two hours to drive to Stanford. I still needed someone to take care of the rest of my kids, so I turned to some of my good friends. I made one more phone call to Tammy Guthrie to ask for help.

All of this was exhausting. Functioning on autopilot, I started cooking macaroni and cheese. By the time the children were sitting down to eat, Tammy had arrived. When she realized I needed to take Bradley all the way to Stanford Children's Hospital, that I wasn't sure where it was, and that I was in no shape to drive anyway, she told me she was going with me then called for more help.

Kathy Stimpson, another friend, arrived minutes later prepared to spend the night at my house. Leaving her own five kids home with her husband was sacrifice enough, but Kathy was nervous about being alone overnight, which made me appreciate her help even more. Kathy's husband, Kerry, and Tammy's husband, Ric, came to give Bradley a priesthood blessing. I felt reassured that whatever we needed to face, we had the help of the Lord to get us through.

I packed a few things for Brad and myself, preparing to stay the rest of the night at the hospital. Tammy and I chose what we thought would be the best route to Stanford and climbed into her station wagon. I held Brad on my lap in the front seat. Normally I am fanatic about my children being in car seats or seat belts. That night I couldn't put Brad down, feeling the need to protect him from whatever unknown disease was waiting to get him. I already felt as if some powerful force was pulling my baby away. I was determined to fight back.

After a forty-five minute drive and a couple of wrong turns, we finally arrived at Stanford at about 8:30 p.m. We went in the front door of the Children's Hospital, entering what appeared to be a deserted building. I carried Bradley, Tammy took our bag of belongings, and we wandered through empty corridors. The whole experience seemed surreal. Finally we found a night janitor who gave us directions to the other end of the hospital.

We weren't alone after all. The oncology staff had been waiting for us to arrive, and a room full of medical personnel quickly descended upon us, appearing somewhat perturbed that I had kept them waiting. Each one asked me the same questions over and over as they took turns inspecting and prodding my sleepy, frightened little boy. After assuring Tammy that I would be all right, I told her to go home before it got any later. I was directed to the check-in desk to take care of insurance and admittance forms. I carried Bradley with me and held him on my lap. The receptionist told me I could put him down while I completed the paper work. She didn't understand that I couldn't let go of him.

After we returned to Brad's room, a nurse stuck an IV needle into his arm and taped a splint underneath to keep him from bending his wrist. She explained he would be given a preliminary dose of chemotherapy. If he did have leukemia, it would be the first dose in his treatment protocol.

After the nurse drew several tubes of blood, the IV drip was started and Brad was settled into the oversize metal hospital crib. I had a cot next to him. When my mom arrived they allowed her to sleep in an empty hospital bed for that first night, even though the rules permitted only one adult to stay overnight.

Brad slept, a "Dukes of Hazard" Matchbox car clutched tightly in each hand. He preferred them to stuffed animals and carried them everywhere he went. His favorite blanket was tucked over him. I lay on my side and watched him sleep, silent tears leaking from my eyes. He was just a tiny little boy. And cancer is such a big thing.

The next morning Bradley stood up in the crib and said firmly, "Get me out of this jail." He had no idea how badly I wanted to do just that. Neither did he realize how aptly he had described his current condition, being held prisoner against his will. Or maybe he did. The nurse had warned me that this would be "The day from hell." What about the day we had just gone through? As she checked Brad's IV line she commented on what pretty blond hair Brad had. I didn't know what to say. All night I had been picturing that hair falling out. Surely she must have known it could soon be gone. Maybe she was so used to seeing bald children that she couldn't help commenting on his hair. I thought it was pretty, too.

I assumed that someone had gotten the girls off to school but was concerned about Nathan who would need someone to watch him the rest of the day. My mom left to go take care of things at home.

A short time later Brad was whisked away by another group of doctors. They seemed to come in packs. Stanford is a teaching hospital, and medical students often accompany doctors as they treat patients. Many tests were yet to be done, including a spinal tap and bone marrow aspiration. Since Bradley had a long day of "pokes" ahead of him, he was anesthetized so that he slept heavily throughout the day. Between procedures, they brought him back into the room, where I had not been alone. The roaming bands of question-asking people continued to visit me, trying to look appropriately pained by my situation. As I recounted the details of Brad's life and my pregnancy with him, I felt like shouting, "I've already told this story to a dozen other people. Can't you just read the charts?" But I answered politely instead.

Wanting to look better than I felt, when Bradley was taken away for more tests, I went to take a shower. Standing under the spray of hot water, I tried to comprehend how my life was suddenly different than just a day ago. I was the mother of a child who probably had cancer. What would it mean for Bradley, for me, for our family? By the time I had dressed and dried and combed my hair I felt a touch braver. Brad was still getting x-rays, which seemed to be taking way too long. I was concerned that something had gone wrong. I tried to occupy myself. I couldn't concentrate on TV or reading, and sleep was out of the question, as was eating. I went for a walk outside, impressed by the hospital's massive, park-like grounds. In different circumstances it could have been very pleasant there.

Dave finally arrived about 2:00 p.m. He had come straight from the airport and had not slept all night. To say he looked awful would be kind. Still, it was a relief for me to have someone to share the stress. I caught him up on the events to that point, and we waited. Our sleepy, sedated son was returned to us a little later. He slept in the crib while I stroked his wavy blond hair. Late in the day a medical team assembled in the room to give us the results of all the tests and a diagnosis. It was leukemia, acute lymphoblastic leukemia (ALL), the most common type of childhood cancer. The good news, the doctors explained, was that it is also the most treatable type of leukemia, with a 70 percent cure rate. Many children were staying in remission and living long lives. We were determined to have a positive outlook and do what was necessary to give Bradley the best chance for survival.

We met Dr. Mitchell, the head of the oncology unit, who answered our questions and explained treatment procedures. Tall, blond, good-looking, and single, the doctor was the source of much admiration among staff and patients alike. He explained that there were currently two nation-wide study groups for treatment of patients with ALL. Brad would be placed at random into one of the groups. Statistics were being compiled to determine which protocol was more successful in keeping patients in remission.

The only major difference between the two studies was the frequency of chemotherapy injections into the spinal fluid. Brad was placed in the group with the less frequent injections. Years later that protocol was discontinued as statistics showed higher success for the children in the other group. It is impossible not to wonder if Brad's life could have been spared through placement in the other group.

Dave and I were given books and pamphlets and more papers to sign. Reading through a list of chemotherapy drugs and their possible side effects, I realized that baldness, while visible, is not the worst side effect; not by a long shot. Each drug had a long list: things like severe nausea, vomiting, mouth ulcers, bleeding from the bladder, depressed platelets which can result in bleeding, liver damage, allergic reaction (occasionally fatal), diarrhea, abdominal pains, GI ulcers, and changes in muscle tone and muscle action. Our child was two years old! How could we possibly subject him to this type of treatment? And yet, how could we not?

Bradley would be receiving intense chemotherapy, to be given through a combination of IV medication, pills, and injections into his spinal fluid (spinal taps or lumbar punctures). He would be on treatment for three years. The first phase of treatment, the induction phase, would take about three months. Then would follow the maintenance phase with lower levels of chemotherapy drugs. At that time he might be cured. I was quickly learning more about leukemia than I had ever wanted to know.

Later that Thursday evening, as the sleepiness from the anesthesia wore off, Bradley began to experience leg pain as a result of a drug he had received. He cried continually through most of the night. He was given a painkiller, but until it took effect he was in agony and lay wincing against my shoulder as I rocked him and tried to soothe him. We both finally fell into an exhausted sleep for a few hours.

Bradley seemed quite cheerful in the morning. When he stood up and I saw his arm, I realized it probably had not been his legs that had caused him so much pain. The IV fluid had infiltrated under his skin instead of going into his vein, and his left arm, from his fingers to above his elbow, was swollen like a fat sausage. It didn't even look like an arm. I was upset with the nurse for not inspecting the IV line sooner. His arm was completely unusable, as he was unable to bend his elbow or his distended fingers. The IV line would have to be placed in his right arm. That meant yet another poke, and a board taped to his dominant arm.

Amazingly, Brad was relatively calm about the whole experience. Unlike the previous two days when the sight of needles had caused him to cry in terror of being poked, he sat quietly throughout the procedure, wincing only a little at the insertion of the needle. It seemed to make him feel better to watch what was happening and have the procedure explained to him. I made frequent inspections of the new IV line, but the problem did not reoccur. It was several days before Brad's arm returned to normal size, and even longer until the bruised coloring of his skin faded.

Friday seemed to mark a bit of a turn-around for Bradley. Up to that point, I had been unable to leave his side for more than a few minutes. He was frightened and did not understand what was happening or why he had to be at a place where everyone seemed to want to hurt him. My mom came each day for a while, and Dave came in the evenings, bringing the other children to visit. But they were able to offer me little relief, since Bradley wouldn't let Grandma hold him at all. He cried for me even when Dave held him, which surprised me, since he had always preferred Dad when given a choice between parents.

Maybe that day he started to feel better, or maybe he just decided to make the best of things. Brad was ready to be a kid again and wanted to play. I put him on the floor with his little cars, and he chased them around the room. It was a real challenge to push the IV pole around and keep up with him.

I also had a turn-around that day, catching a glimmer of hope that Brad might still have a happy, somewhat normal childhood. Another mom came to our room and asked if I would like to talk. Her name was Debbie, the mother of a five-year-old whirlwind, who just happened to be a leukemia patient. I had noticed him earlier when walking the halls and grounds. Tyler didn't have ALL. He had AML, acute myelocytic leukemia, which at that time was incurable. He had already lived two years since diagnosis, longer than predicted. But his life was not over yet. Since cancer had brought him and his family to this place, they were making the most of it.

As soon as his chemo was done, Tyler was disconnected from his IV line and dashed outside. Tyler had a bicycle at the hospital. The minute he was free, he strapped a helmet onto his bald head and took off, pedaling full speed around the sidewalks. He had a child-sized tent that Debbie had put up for him on the lawn, filled with toys to entertain him and his younger brother. Brad was invited to play there any time. Watching Tyler was amazing. It was impossible to see him fly past and not smile. If this child could be happy, have energy, and enjoy life, maybe Brad could too.

"Are there ever any really good days?" I asked Debbie cautiously. "You know, days when you forget about cancer and feel like normal people?"

"Absolutely," she reassured me. "They're almost all good."

One concern that had no resolution was the question of "why?" Why had Bradley contracted leukemia? We had four other healthy children who shared the same physical environment and had many of the same genetic factors as Brad. Since the cause of leukemia was unknown, I wondered if I had somehow contributed to Brad's illness. Was he being made sick by something he ate, drank, wore, or slept on? Was it the paint on our walls or the type of laundry soap we used? Was it the high voltage power lines that ran overhead a few blocks from our house? It was very disturbing to think that we might be continuing to expose Brad to the very thing that had caused his disease.

Even in those days of learning to cope with the new diagnosis of leukemia, I began to find "treasures in the sand." I learned just how wonderful our friends were and how much we needed them. The friends at home and the new ones at the hospital all helped our family cope, physically as well as emotionally.

I began to look at life with a new perspective. Each day suddenly became a precious commodity to be used wisely and remembered for its goodness. When the possibility of death hangs over life, especially a young life, it is easy to sort out the things that are important.

Chapter 4

FACING THE WORLD

On Monday morning Dr. Mitchell announced that Bradley was ready to go home. I received this news with mixed emotions. Of course I looked forward to getting out of the hospital and being back together with the rest of the family, but I was nervous about the responsibility of taking over Brad's care. Each day he would be taking several medications, whose names I could not yet pronounce. I worried about side effects, about Brad's susceptibility to communicable illnesses, and about my own ability to face people. The only visitors who had come to see us at the hospital were Dave, my mom, and our other children. The protective bubble of the hospital had kept us isolated from the questions of well-meaning friends and the eyes of the curious.

Nurses patiently explained procedures to follow at home, and doctors detailed the medication schedule. We loaded a toy wagon to transport our accumulated possessions to the car. Even though we had come with only a change of clothes, we had a considerable amount of stuff to cart out. There were the additional supplies I had requested Mom or Dave to bring from home, gifts that Brad had received, and hospital supplies. You get to take home your tissue, your plastic container (affectionately known as the "barf bucket"), and any other items that have been opened for your benefit but not consumed. Dave and I loaded all this and Bradley into our van and headed off to face the next phase of our lives.

It seemed impossible that the rest of the world was unchanged in the five days that had turned our lives upside down. It was strange to see people jogging and riding bikes on the trail behind the hospital, just like when things were normal. Springtime in the Santa Clara Valley is stunning, and it starts in February. As we drove home along Interstate 280, the grass on the hillsides was a brilliant green, accented with colorful wild flowers. All this beauty seemed like a sign of hope. I tried not to feel guilty that I enjoyed it.

Our friend, Laurie Marquis, had known we were coming home that day. She had left a bag of food on our porch so we wouldn't have to prepare dinner. The bag contained all the ingredients and assembly instructions for "Spoon Tacos," a type of taco salad. Our kids loved it, and it became a favorite family meal.

I needed help from my friends on a regular basis. Bradley had to go back to Stanford at least once a week for blood tests, IV chemotherapy infusions, and check-ups. There were some medications that required an overnight stay at the hospital. One series of shots had to be given daily for five consecutive days. My friends and I had always traded baby-sitting, since many of us in the neighborhood had small children. After Brad got sick, they baby-sat far more times than I could ever repay.

When Dave was in town and could get away from work, he took Brad for chemotherapy so I could stay home and take care of the other children. This was especially helpful during the summer when school was out and I needed to take the four older kids along for Brad's appointments. It was also a welcome break for me when Dave took Brad to the hospital. Just being with him for his routine treatments was physically and emotionally exhausting.

A typical hospital day went something like this: all five kids got up, ate breakfast, and got dressed. I combed five heads of hair (four after Brad went bald), and then took the girls to school. If it was a preschool day, I dropped Nathan off early at the home where preschool was being held. One of the other moms would take Nathan home after preschool, and Laurie picked up the girls after school and took them to her house until I got home.

Brad and I had to stop at our medical insurance office before every appointment to get authorization of payment for that day's treatment. This went on for a number of weeks before they finally decided they could give us authorization for several visits on a single form. The difficulties with insurance companies plagued us throughout the years of Brad's illness, adding a great deal of stress to an already taxing situation. We knew we were very fortunate, though, to have good medical coverage, which paid the majority of expenses for his treatment.

Our first outpatient visit to the oncology clinic was like walking into a horror ride at an amusement park. "STOP!" "CAUTION!" "GO BACK!" "DO NOT ENTER IF YOU HAVE BEEN EXPOSED TO CHICKEN POX!" Oh dear. I didn't think we had been exposed but the signs made me nervous. Chicken pox posed a deadly threat to children with weakened immune systems. Brad and our other children had all had chicken pox one year earlier. But what if there was an outbreak in our neighborhood that we had been exposed to and we unknowingly had little chicken pox germs clinging to us? I didn't want that responsibility.

The first time I read the sign, "Hematology, Oncology," at the entrance to the outpatient clinic, it hit me again that we were really dealing with cancer. I wished that we were there for hematology, or better yet, not there at all. Were people staring? Were they thinking, "Oh, that poor little boy must have cancer." Well, the whole situation basically stank. It was a perfectly nice spring day, and we should have been out playing at a park. I watched the bikers and joggers on the nearby path, healthy, healthy, healthy. I felt cheated,

Brad was cheated. He loved being a little boy, banging on stuff with a hammer, body slamming his big brother.

The carefreeness of childhood had drained out of Brad into the IV lines during his initial stay at the hospital. Since he could no longer assume life would be all fun and games, he decided to do what he could to take control of things. Almost overnight he took on more grown-up roles. He had not been much of a talker. Now he talked non-stop, especially to ask questions about his care and to inform nurses of the proper procedures. He learned the type and size of needle he liked for having blood drawn and getting IV infusions. He was adamant about choosing the vein in which the needle should be placed. He had favorite veins inside the joint of the elbow of each arm, which never changed over the next fourteen years. Phlebotomists often tried to convince him that those veins were worn out and another one would work better. He told them to try one of his favorites first. Wonder of wonders, those veins never failed.

As long as Bradley could watch what was being done, ask about the medications, and supervise the whole process, he never cried. He whimpered in anticipation of the dreaded "leg pokes" but sat still to get it over with. The only procedures he really hated were "back pokes." These included lumbar punctures (spinal taps) and bone marrow aspirations. He had both of these every two weeks during the induction phase of treatment. They are very painful, especially the bone marrow aspirations, which have been compared to having the inside of your bones sucked out through a straw. At Stanford they sedated him to lessen the pain. I wondered, though, if they had given him a mirror so he could see what was being done, if maybe he would have been fine without the sedative.

Days at the clinic included lots of waiting. We had to wait to get blood drawn, wait for the results of the blood test, wait to get a check-up, wait for medications to be ordered and arrive from the pharmacy, wait for a nurse to start an IV drip, then wait for the IV to run its course, which varied from one to about four hours. Brad played in the courtyard or the playroom with bald, puffy children, some of whom were amputees. Moms and dads sat in the waiting room, reading, knitting, and staring. There was some talking between parents. Some seemed unable to shut up, spewing out details of their child's condition, or jabbering away about things completely unrelated. Most just wanted to get through the day, hope for good results, and move on to more mundane things. The time I wasn't directly involved with Brad, I chose to spend reading. It was a great escape from reality. I didn't want to get too close to the other parents, knowing that if we became friends I would have to experience some of their pain. I already had enough of my own.

In the clinic, however, we often saw the same parents and children week after week because we were on similar treatment schedules. In conversations with other parents, I learned how they were dealing with cancer and how it was changing their lives. One mom told me about her recent divorce, a result of the stress, and her need to now accept welfare in order to pay medical bills. In some families where both parents had been working, one of them had been forced to quit their job in order to be full time with their sick child, causing serious financial strain.

It was interesting that most parents were very open about their dependence on God to help them face their trials. It seemed that a crisis like cancer either made people turn to their religious background for strength or completely loose faith. Some could not accept that such a horrible thing could happen to innocent children if God cared about them. But most people realized that they needed strength beyond their own and found comfort and peace through their faith. Dave and I were extremely grateful for our understanding of the eternal nature of life and the knowledge that we, and Brad, were being watched over by a loving Heavenly Father. We could not imagine the emptiness of facing such trials without that reassurance.

The children in the clinic constantly amazed me. Whether they were in wheelchairs, trailing IV poles, or limping along on prosthesis, they were happy kids. They played together, smiling at the nurses who came to get them for what would inevitably be painful experiences. The sound of crying coming from a treatment room was not uncommon, but neither was the sound of laughter. They were not cancer patients who happened to be kids. They were kids who happened to have cancer. It was an inconvenience that interrupted their childhood but did not define it.

One thing that Brad always looked forward to was a visit to the Big Red Toy Chest. After enduring difficult procedures such as back pokes, he was allowed to look through the contents of the chest and choose any toy he wanted to take home and keep. Brad was thrilled to find "He Man" figures among the choices. These hideous figures of men-beast combinations were very popular at the time, and were so ugly that I would never have bought them for him. He chose a different one each visit, until he had collected at least one or two of every variety.

When Bradley's treatment required an overnight stay, we tried to schedule it for a Friday night so that Dave could be home with the other kids. The patient rooms at that time all accommodated two patients, with the exception of isolation units. He had been in an isolation room during his initial stay at diagnosis, both for his own protection from infection and out of consideration for our privacy at that tumultuous time.

During one overnight stay we shared a room with a teenage cancer patient. He was very ill and never left his bed. His mother talked to me briefly as she left the room from time to time, as we were on the side near the door. During evening visiting hours a number of high school students came to see our roommate. They looked like cheerleaders and athletes, well-groomed young people with everything going for them. The curtain drawn through the center of the room separated them from view, but I could hear their upbeat, though quiet, conversation with their sick friend. They told him about what was going on at school, joked, and made him laugh. After visiting awhile, they told him they would be back and left quietly.

I thought about the young man in the next bed. Had he been a football or basketball player? Was he a class officer? Or was he just a good kid that other people truly cared about? I know he was in pain. I could hear him whispering to his mom during the night and her softly reassuring him. Though his discomfort seemed to keep him awake all night, he was considerate and tried to avoid disturbing Bradley and me.

About a week later I was in the waiting room of the clinic for Brad's regular appointment when I saw the boy's mother. I said hello and asked if they were there for a check-up. She said no, that her son would probably need to be admitted. Then I saw him, not standing, or even sitting in a wheel chair, but lying on a gurney. I knew he was dying. His brave mother smiled at me, and I wished I had known what to say. She must have been a single mother, since the boy's father was not there that day nor when we had shared the room. Maybe he was her only child, her whole family. I wish I had told her how much I admired her son, and that he must be someone really special to have such great friends. We never saw them again at the hospital.

Chapter 5

GOING BALD

The first week back home I was very nervous about taking Brad to public places. We had been warned that as a result of receiving chemotherapy, his resistance to disease would be low. With four other children bringing the latest communicable illness into our home on a regular basis, he could be exposed to something without even leaving the house. It was tempting, but not practical, to become reclusive. Gradually, we resumed most of our regular activities. I found that keeping to our familiar routines gave us a sense of security. We couldn't alter the fact that Bradley had leukemia, but we could retain control of other aspects of our lives.

That first Sunday after leaving the hospital, we went to church and sat in our usual place on the front row of the chapel. Brad was sitting on my lap, as I made an effort to protect him from the germs that I could almost see flying around the room. A child on the row right behind us had a cold. Every time he coughed or sneezed, I wanted to turn around and tell his mother to take him home, that he was spreading germs that would make Bradley even more sick. Ultimately, though, I need not have worried. Brad did not catch a cold. In fact, he rarely got sick through his years of treatment. That made it possible for us to avoid making leukemia the chief focus of our lives.

Every day I carefully and somewhat fearfully examined Bradley for side effects of chemotherapy. After a couple of weeks on treatment when he had not lost any of his hair, I was convinced he was going to escape that trauma. During a visit to the hospital, I mentioned to a nurse that Brad had not lost any hair and that I was sure he would be an exception and not lose it at all. "He'll lose it," she replied. "It just takes awhile." Sure enough, that very week I started to notice hair in his crib in the mornings. When I gave him a bath, it came off in my hands. He looked like a shedding dog when it fell onto his clothing. But losing his hair was a long process. There is a lot of hair on a person's head, and it was several days before he started to look bald.

About that same time he was taking his first round of a steroid called prednisone. Its side effects include weight gain, both from increased appetite and from water retention. His cheeks puffed up, just like the children I had observed in the waiting room, and his pants became too tight around his waist. He was hungry all the time and had a craving for protein. He wanted meat, and if that was not available, he would settle for cheese or something starchy like left-over potatoes.

I was very protective of Brad as his appearance changed, becoming overly sensitive to the stares and comments of others. At church he was getting a drink in the fountain when I overheard children whispering, "Look at Brad! He's bald!" Adults didn't say anything within my hearing, but their faces made the same comments that the children said out loud. I still wasn't ready to admit he was bald. He had some hair left, thin wisps that attracted static electricity and tended to fly at odd angles from his head like a miniature Albert Einstein. I knew I should shave off the stragglers, but I couldn't bring myself to do that. When at last the hair was gone, I was surprised to find I actually liked his baldness. He had a smooth, round head that was fun to rub, especially when new hair fuzz started to come in and it felt like velvet stubble.

Bradley liked the fact that he didn't need to have his hair combed. And he got new hats. He didn't mind having his head bare, but sunburn was a concern, its effect magnified by drug reactions. Hats protected him and became part of his identity. He received hats for gifts and from the toy chest at the hospital; a collection began to grow.

When he was bald during fourth grade his favorite hat was a black baseball cap with multicolored circles scattered over it. On his Make-A-Wish trip to Disney World, he got a florescent green hat that became the new hat of choice. During his teenage years Brad liked to wear the bandanna-type head coverings that were popular among snowboarders. I let him wear them only to the hospital or cancer related activities, since I wasn't fond of them.

One time after Brad's hair grew back in, it was getting long enough to require combing. He was about ten at the time and begged me to shave it off again so he wouldn't have to comb it. I told him there was not a chance I would shave his head. He had earned that hair back and had just better learn to enjoy it. So he did. He spent more time then his sisters in front of the bathroom mirror, experimenting with styling gel and hair spray. He wanted his hair in the current style and was very disappointed that it never got thick enough for an impressive bowl cut when they were popular.

Janene got a hat for Christmas one year with the words "Bad Hair Day" stitched on the front. Brad loved that hat, begged to borrow it on a regular basis, finally just taking over ownership. It was the one he wore almost constantly during the final year of his life.

The only time I ever saw Brad get his feelings hurt over being bald happened soon after the first time he lost his hair. I was driving Nathan's car pool for preschool, and one of the four-year-old boys teased him about it. Brad turned on him and said, "You just be quiet. I have a sickness that makes my hair fall out, and I can't help it." It surprised me that Brad remembered that incident years later. He didn't forget how hurtful that experience was. Fortunately, almost everyone else who knew him was very kind. He had friends of all ages that loved and defended him.

Once we were shopping in a department store when a middle-aged lady exclaimed, "What a cute little boy! How old is he?"

"Three," I replied.

"Oh, he looks younger since he's just getting his hair. All my babies were born bald and didn't grow hair until they were at least two," continued the shopper.

"Yes, his hair is just coming in," I said. Sometimes it was not worth telling the whole story to strangers.

THE LIFE STORY OF MY HAIR, By Bradley Coles
September 16, 1998

I was born without hair but I was told it grew quickly by the time I was nine months old. When I was two, though, I got cancer and lost all of it to chemotherapy. It grew back a little again and again, but I lost all of it when I was in first grade. People bugged me about it, but it never really got to me. The other times it did fall out were when I was in fourth grade, in the summer of my fifth grade year, and in my eighth grade year at school.

I never did have really long or thick hair. I think I am glad it never got that way because it makes it hard to comb. Right now my hair is pretty much all in and I don't think that it will fall out for quite some time, at least I hope not. It's hard to comb my hair when it is falling out.

Chapter 6

NORMAL FAMILY AGAIN

As the summer of 1985 approached, we began thinking of a place we might go for our family vacation. It needed to be special, memorable. We had already learned an important lesson from leukemia, and that was to live life to the fullest. I learned to ask myself, "Am I going to regret this later?" That applied to things I did as well as opportunities I chose to pass up. I was becoming a better parent and a better person as I looked at things with a new perspective of what is important. We spent time together with our family whenever possible. After talking about some possible vacation destinations, we decided on a trip up the Oregon coast, continuing north to Seattle, then to Vancouver and Victoria, British Colombia. We were excited about our plans, but nervous about taking Bradley so far from home.

The doctors gave us permission to travel, but that did not make me entirely at ease. The farthest we had gone since his diagnosis was to my parents' home near Sacramento, where plenty of medical help was available if needed. The coast of Oregon has miles of space far from any sizable town. That was part of the appeal. The trip would test whether we could be a normal family and go where we wanted. Bradley had completed his induction phase of chemotherapy at the end of June. It had taken over four months instead of the predicted three, because of being "bumped" from treatment a few times. The term "bumped" means that after having a blood test, the patient is found to have low counts in some aspect of the blood chemistry, which makes chemotherapy too risky at that time. Being bumped is always a cause for concern, since abnormal blood counts can indicate relapse. Overall, Bradley had done very well with the treatments. The leukemia went into remission, as predicted and hoped for. Other than the side effects of chemotherapy, he had been healthy.

We planned to be gone for about ten days on our trip, which meant Brad would miss a scheduled chemotherapy infusion. He had been at the hospital at least once a week since February. I worried that missing one day of scheduled treatment would cause a relapse. To appease my concerns, we scheduled Brad's appointment for late in the week before we left, and early on the week of our return to shorten the time away by a few days. Dr. Mitchell gave us the names of doctors in Portland and Seattle to contact if Brad had problems near those cities. All of the medical staff encouraged us to take the trip, promising it would be good for our whole family.

The itinerary we chose was ambitious. Budget restrictions meant we would be camping. We stayed only at campgrounds with hot showers and flush toilets, my minimum daily requirements for remaining human. I made the reservations before we left home so we were assured of a place to stay each night. After arriving at a campground, we went to work, setting up our large tent and preparing dinner. We unrolled sleeping bags and piled on extra blankets against the chilly, damp weather. After a picnic dinner and some time on the playground, I took the three girls and Brad to have showers and get ready for bed. Nathan went with Dave to the guys' bathroom to shower. In the mornings we got everyone dressed, rolled up the sleeping bags, took down the tent, and fixed breakfast. It was time consuming, but it saved money and the kids loved camping.

As we drove farther northward, my cares seemed to stay behind. We were a normal family again, off on a summer adventure. Brad's bald head and puffy appearance aside, we felt free. We climbed sand dunes and picked wild berries, then searched for treasures on wind swept beaches. There were stops at cheese factories and fisheries. At Fort Clatsop our children became explorers as they donned period attire and watched soldiers fire the muskets. In Seattle we enjoyed the view from the top of the Space Needle and rode the Monorail. We crossed the border into Canada and took a ferry to Vancouver Island where we strolled Butchart Gardens. It was a great trip. We returned home knowing that leukemia didn't have to be the main focus of our lives.

Chapter 7

NEW HOME IN UTAH

In September 1985 Dave was offered employment with a company in Salt Lake City. Before accepting the position, Dave and I took Brad to Utah to meet with doctors at Primary Children's Hospital. We wanted to be sure he would continue to receive the same quality of care he was getting at Stanford.

We scheduled an appointment with Dr. Roberts, the head of the oncology department. Primary Children's Hospital, located near the state capitol, was an imposing brick structure perched on a hill overlooking the Salt Lake Valley. We located the oncology outpatient clinic and explained to the receptionist that we had an appointment to meet with Dr. Roberts. Soon a short, stocky, dark-haired guy wearing Birkenstock sandals invited us into his office. His manner was friendly, but direct. We reviewed Brad's medical history and treatment protocol. The doctor assured us that the exact schedule of medications could be maintained in Utah.

At the end of our visit, we felt comfortable that the doctors at Primary Children's Hospital would provide Brad with the necessary medical care. We reviewed the insurance policy that came with the job offer, and it seemed acceptable. At random I selected a pediatrician from the list of doctors on the plan and made an appointment to take Brad in as soon as we moved.

Our family arrived in Utah the first week in November. Monday morning I enrolled the other kids in school and took Brad to meet his new pediatrician. Dr.

Jensen was a pleasant man who had ties to Stanford and was close friends with one of the oncologists at Primary Children's Hospital. I was happy with the outcome of my random choice of doctors.

Our new neighborhood was filled with kids. After we settled into the house and bought appropriate clothing for the climate, the children found new friends and started to feel at home. Brad and I had lots of time together during the hours everyone else was at school. He was a kid that I could take anywhere. He sat quietly through PTA meetings, playing with Matchbox cars or coloring. When I had church responsibilities, he would tag along quite happily and sit on my lap without causing a disturbance. He was a cheerful companion on shopping trips, whether riding in a cart through a grocery store or in the stroller at a mall.

Brad quickly made friends with the staff at his new hospital. He liked to joke with Dr. Roberts and was a little disappointed if another doctor gave him his check-ups. He looked forward to seeing the nurses, especially Jodie and Sarah. At Stanford, Bradley had been having bone marrow aspirations every two months since he had started maintenance protocol, to monitor whether he was staying in remission. At Primary Children's, they were done only if a relapse was suspected. When he received "back pokes" at Stanford, Bradley was sedated, and felt tired the rest of the day. In Utah, we were urged to have him try the procedures without sedatives. I let Brad choose. He weighed the pros and cons and decided he would rather suffer through a few minutes of pain than be asleep the rest of the day and miss out on something fun. He began having the procedures done without medication.

In January of 1986, Bradley started attending the Newcastle Preschool, located right across the street from our house. Our neighbor, Kathleen Jensen, was the school director. Brad loved having "Miss Kaf-leen" for his teacher. Most of the students at the school lived nearby and Brad made friends with them. He was open about the fact that he had cancer, that sometimes his hair came out, and sometimes he took medicine that made him look fat. The other kids were okay with that, curious but not judgmental. Once he started preschool, Brad always wanted to play with friends instead of just being at home with me. He became somewhat of a ladies' man, preferring girls to boys when there was a choice.

Our first summer in Utah, Dave and I decided to take the family on a trip to visit some of the National Parks in the southern part of our new state. The plan was to visit Bryce Canyon, Zion National Park, and the north rim of the Grand Canyon.

The first day, we went to Bryce Canyon. Driving along the park's main road, we pulled out at many of the vista points and took short hikes to see the rock formations, carved by centuries of erosion into fantastic shapes. As we walked back up the path from yet another incredible overlook, Bradley sighed, then said, "I wish you would have brought some other kid instead of me."

He didn't whine or complain, but he had made a point. I could already tell that dragging five kids in and out of the van dozens of times a day to look at rocks was going to make for a long week. I turned to Dave and suggested, "Let's go to Disneyland."

"Are you serious?"

"Yes, let's do it. We'll drive through Zion National Park tomorrow, make a quick stop at the North Rim of the Grand Canyon the next day, then head to California for the rest of the week."

There was much cheering from the back of the van. We all loved Disneyland. Dave's parents lived only an hour's drive from there, so we would have a place to stay. Thanks to Brad, we all enjoyed a much more kid-friendly vacation.

Brad started kindergarten in the fall of 1987 at Quail Hollow Elementary. He went to the morning session and had Mrs. Zimowski as his teacher. He, along with most of the other five-year-olds, pronounced it "Miss Mouskey." Four of our children attended Quail Hollow Elementary School that year. Alisa, our oldest child was in seventh grade at Albion Middle School. I was vice president/president elect of Quail Hollow's PTA that year. As such, I was at school almost as many days a week as our children.

Bradley walked to school every morning with his siblings, and I picked him up after kindergarten. As the year progressed, he convinced me to let him walk home with his friends. I could see nearly all the way to the school from our house so it was a safe walk. I often waited outside for him to come down the street. He had to miss school at least once every two weeks for chemotherapy and a check-up. Every day after school he wanted to play with someone. Tiring of looking up phone numbers for him, I wrote a list of his friends' names and phone numbers. It was not long before he had memorized the ten numbers on the list.

Jonathan Roatcap moved in two blocks up the street and became Brad's best friend. Their favorite thing to play with was toy swords. Some of Brad's swords came with a belt and a holster that he wore to carry them to Jonathan's house. If there was no holster, he improvised and just stuck the sword in the back of his pants. He ran all over the neighborhood on his short little legs, a sword protruding from his waistband. He liked to wear "moon boots," his pull-on snow boots, even in summer, since they had no laces to tie and he could put them on by himself. T-shirt, shorts, moon boots, and a sword; it was quite an outfit.

The first girl that Brad had a crush on was Ivy Gillespie. She was a cute little blond who liked to giggle as much as Brad did. Brad's first phone call in his daily search for someone to play with was usually to Ivy, even before Jonathan.

From Brad's Journal, October 4, 1987

I like going to school. I am in kindergarten now. My teacher is Mrs. Zimowski. I like playing with my friends and playing at recess and watching movies. Some of my friends are Jonathan, Bobby, Scott, Valerie, and Natalie. I have still some other friends, but I don't know their names.

Brad's Journal Entry, March 27, 1988

I go to soccer now. It's fun. We learned how to dribble the ball with our feet. I am taking ice skating lessons. It's fun. We bend our knees and put our arms out. I can go backwards and frontwards. I can stop by pushing my feet out to the sides.

I am real good at riding my bike now. We went for a bike ride yesterday, and I got to ride my own bike instead of riding on the back of Daddy's bike. We went for a long ride.

I am almost done taking my medicines now. Pretty soon I won't have to take any more.

This was a very happy period of time for our family. We found many things to love about our new home state, especially the nearby mountains where we could picnic and hike or just throw rocks into the streams. New friends were filling in the gaps created when we moved from San Jose. I sometimes wished that I could freeze our lives at that stage forever. Bradley was out of diapers and in remission; Alisa was not yet a teenager. What more could a mom ask for? While our kids had their share of disagreements they were usually kind to each other. We had a new home, new friends, and renewed hope for the future, as Brad neared the end of his chemotherapy.

Brad, Nathan, and Michael Weiss eating breakfast at the Fathers' and Sons' campout in July 1988

Chapter 8

NO MORE BACK POKES

It was April 1988. Three years and two months had passed since Bradley's diagnosis of leukemia. He would finish his last chemotherapy before his sixth birthday. As we neared the end of his scheduled treatments, I began to worry. He was doing so well on treatment it seemed logical to me that he stay on low levels of chemotherapy indefinitely. When I discussed this with the doctors, they assured me that he was ready to be drug free. If a relapse was going to occur, it would happen eventually even if he continued on treatment, and the poisonous effects of continuing chemotherapy would damage his body in other ways.

The oncology clinic at Primary Children's Hospital held a little celebration whenever a patient completed the last day of cancer treatment. Brad had seen other kids leave with happy congratulations and toys and was looking forward to his turn. I had reservations about celebrating too much. Something in the back of my mind wouldn't let me believe it was really over. Brad would still need to have a check-up every three months for a year, then once a year for five years. At that point if all went well, he would be considered cancer free. That was the case for about 70 percent of patients with acute lymphoblastic leukemia. We knew the statistics. I also knew that a lot of the kids being treated at the hospital were relapse patients.

Brad passed his check-up with flying colors. Blood tests were normal, his health was great; a happy ending to three plus years of fear and suffering. For some reason, no one seemed to realize it was Brad's final chemotherapy day. I mentioned it to a nurse, who was apologetic that it had slipped past their attention. She scrounged around and found him a teddy bear as a gift. He was told he would never need to have any more back pokes, not ever. That, to Bradley, was the best gift of all.

It was very strange to put Brad to bed that night without any medication. It made me nervous. He had taken pills at least once a day during the whole course of treatment. Stopping the drugs cold turkey seemed to me like an invitation for trouble, even though I knew it was standard protocol.

About a week later, Brad began to get a rash all over his arms. I took him to see Dr. Jensen, our pediatrician, who diagnosed eczema and told me not to give him baths every day, as it was drying his skin. I asked if the rash might be a reaction to stopping the drugs to which his system had become accustomed, but the doctor felt that was very unlikely. Still, the fact that he had suddenly developed a condition that had never before affected him or any member of our family seemed like more than a coincidence of timing. Treating the rash as the doctor directed resulted in little improvement.

Brad had been off treatment nearly three weeks when he started having headaches---bad ones. Even with pain relievers he had difficulty sleeping. I feared it could be a relapse and called our pediatrician again for advice. He had me bring Brad into his office and did a blood test, which showed no abnormalities. Dr. Jensen thought it could be a migraine, and assured me that even young children can get them especially if they experience stress. I cautiously brought up the possibility of relapse. He admitted it was a possible cause of the headaches, but Brad looked healthy, and the blood test seemed to rule out leukemia.

The morning after the doctor's appointment, Brad said his head hurt, but not too badly. He wanted to go to school. I reluctantly consented to let him go, with the agreement that he would call me if he did not feel well. I was anxious all morning, waiting for the phone to ring, but it didn't. I started to relax, assuming he must be feeling better. When it was time for kindergarten to get out for the day I watched Brad's friends come down the street. He wasn't with them. Becoming concerned, I drove to the school, expecting to meet him along the way. There was no sign of him. Trying to keep calm, I reasoned he was probably in the office waiting for a turn to use the phone and call me to pick him up.

After parking, I headed into the front door of the school, passing the kindergarten playground. There, lying face down on the gravel, holding his head in his hands, was Brad. I asked him why he hadn't called me. He said that his head hurt too much to move. I gently helped him up, feeling like the world's worst mom. How could I have let him go to school? I knew he was now in serious pain, and the implications of that. I called Dave at work and asked him to meet us at the hospital.

It was awful, walking back into the clinic where less than a month before Brad had been given a clean bill of health. Now he needed to have a full series of tests done to determine the cause of his head pain, tests that included a spinal tap and bone marrow aspiration. When Brad heard what the doctor was going to do, he looked at me with hurt-filled eyes and said, "But they told me I would never have any more back pokes," and started to cry. It was almost more that I could take, and I passed my own frustration on to the medical staff, telling them they had been foolish for making him a promise that now could not be kept.

Fortunately, Dave held himself together and calmly told me that he was going with Brad to get the tests done, and I could wait outside the room if I didn't want to come. As he and Brad left with the doctor, I realized that being upset was of no value to anyone, especially Brad. He was going to face the procedures whether or not I was there to offer reassurance and comfort. Forcing myself to regain control, I went to the next room and took Brad's hand as he once again prepared to have the marrow of his bones extracted through a syringe.

As soon as Bradley finished the spinal tap, his head quit hurting. While Dave and I sat with him in the waiting room, he felt well enough to play with the toys and asked for something to eat. We must have overreacted, I reasoned. He was going to be fine. Then Dr. Short, one of the oncologists, came to get us to discuss the test results. The look on his face, and the fact that we were ushered into a private room, told me what I didn't want to hear. The spinal fluid contained a large number of leukemia or "blast" cells. Brad had relapsed. It was a CNS, or central nervous system relapse, which explained the headaches. The blast cells increased the volume of fluid in the spinal column and put pressure on his brain. When the spinal tap released some of the pressure, he had instantly felt better.

There was no evidence of leukemia in his bone marrow, which was a big plus. According to statistics he still had a fifty-fifty chance of long-term survival with conventional chemotherapy and radiation to his cranial/spinal region. I asked Dr. Short and Dr. Roberts about the possibility of Brad having a bone marrow transplant. From my research I knew, while very risky and often not successful, transplants were working well for a small number of patients. The doctors felt that Brad had at least as good a chance of cure with standard treatment as he would with a transplant. It was still a very experimental procedure at that time. They discouraged us from pursuing that option. Bradley would start on a "reinduction" phase of chemotherapy immediately, but did not need to be admitted to the hospital.

We left the clinic about the same time our older children were getting out of school. They had no warning of the news we had to share with them and were devastated by it. I was Janene's Brownie Scout leader, and we had a field trip scheduled for that afternoon. I debated whether to hurry and call everyone to cancel, or go ahead with the field trip. It actually seemed easier to take the girls to see the historic buildings we were planning to visit than to call all the parents and explain my reason for canceling. Dave had come home instead of returning to work, so he went along to give me moral support. Brad was now feeling back to normal, and we took him on the walking tour with us. Afterwards, he ran up and down the hills at a park with Janene and the other girls. It was comforting to see that he was very much alive and showed no signs of letting leukemia get the best of him.

The second round of chemotherapy caused Brad more difficulties than the first series. He still managed to go to school and finish kindergarten. During the summer he was tired a lot and had problems with his digestive system. One of the side effects that troubled him the most was mouth sores. There were red, open sores all over his mouth and as far down his throat as we could see. The fact that he was having stomach pain and bleeding stools made it evident that the sores went throughout his digestive system. Chemotherapy kills all the fast growing cells in the body. The hope is that it will eradicate the fast growing cancer cells, but it is not selective. Like hair follicles, the cells on the inside of the mouth and digestive track regenerate quickly and are thus subject to destruction by chemotherapy.

Along with the mouth sores, Brad began to run a fever. We were instructed to contact the hospital any time his temperature exceeded 101 degrees Fahrenheit. Anything lower could be treated at home; a higher temperature required hospitalization. Twice during that summer Bradley's temperature went too high, and he was admitted to the hospital. He was given IV antibiotics as a necessary precaution against infection. It was also a way to get nutrients into him, as he had stopped eating. The drugs altered the taste of food and made it unpleasant. His mouth sores hurt worse when he tried to eat.

For three days during his first hospitalization that summer all we could convince him to eat was an occasional nibble of a graham cracker. I asked him for the hundredth time if there was anything he felt like eating---a milkshake, some juice, Jell-O, a Popsicle. Out of the blue, Brad said he thought he could eat some bacon. I explained to him that because it was salty it might hurt his throat. But it was the only thing that sounded good to him.

Though it was well past breakfast time, Brad's nurse pleaded his case to a reluctant kitchen staff and his bacon was delivered. I was amazed when he ate not just a nibble, but all four pieces. Two more times during that day he got a bacon craving. Two more times, with medical recommendations from the nurses, the bacon was ordered and consumed. By the next day he was eating normally and the sores began to heal. Now, I don't believe there are any magical healing properties in bacon. In fact, it is probably one of the least nutritious foods available. But I do believe that patients know their bodies better than anyone. I am grateful for kind nurses who went out of their way to get bacon for a sick little boy in spite of their medical qualms about the wisdom of that choice. It was what he needed, whether psychologically or physically. We went home within forty-eight hours of the first bacon serving.

Brad was hospitalized one other time that summer because of low blood counts. He had the back half of a two-patient room. A little boy from Idaho was in the other bed. He had been seriously injured when a parked fishing boat fell off its support and landed on his legs. His parents were not able to stay with him, and he was often lonely, demanding lots of attention from the nurses. I was glad that we lived close enough to the hospital that when Bradley had to stay there Dave or I could be with him all the time.

Sleeping arrangements for parents at the old Primary Children's Hospital were dismally inadequate. A recliner chair, which was supposed to fold out flat but didn't, was placed next to each patient's bed. They were old and made of ugly brown vinyl. There were blankets available to make sort of a bed on the chair, which was squished into a corner of the cramped room. I was never able to sleep on the chairs. They were too short to stretch out on, and the blankets slid off the vinyl. Dave, who can sleep anywhere, usually took the night shift.

I stayed with Bradley all day. Dave came directly to the hospital from work. I would then go home, make dinner and take care of the other kids, drive them to lessons, do the housework, and sometimes take the kids back to the hospital for a visit with Brad during the evening. In the morning, I returned to the hospital with a clean change of clothes for Dave, and he went back to work. The older children were now old enough to be left home without babysitters. I still hated to leave them alone all day during the summer or in the hours after school. Fortunately, Bradley's hospital stays were infrequent and usually not more than about five days long.

One day when Brad and I were at the clinic for chemotherapy, a university student asked me to answer questions for a research paper she was writing about the ways in which cancer disrupts family life. She asked me what the hardest time had been. Without hesitation I replied it had been the first relapse. Before the relapse, our hope was that Bradley would be cured, and cancer would become a memory. When he relapsed, we knew he could loose the battle.

Brad's Journal Entry, October 23, 1988

We have been very busy. When I was still in kindergarten my cancer came back. I had to go to the hospital a lot of times. My hair all fell out again. Sometimes the medicines made me throw up. I feel good now, and my hair is coming back. But I have to take some more medicines and it will fall out again.

In the summer we did some fun things. We went to some cabins to stay overnight. Carolyn and her kids came up with Grandma and Grandpa the next day. We went boating and fishing on the lake there. Kristi and Tyler got in a boat with no paddles and floated away, but they floated over to the side.

We went to Grandma and Grandpa Taylor's and swam and went water skiing. Sometimes in the summer I had to stay in the hospital. I hate it there. They give me shots.

We went to a family reunion in Idaho with Grandma and Grandpa Coles and some of my cousins. There was a big swimming pool and some water slides. We camped in our tent. There was a skunk by the building. Grandpa put a garbage can over it and carried it away.

Our best vacation was going to Hawaii. We got there in three airplanes. I liked swimming in the ocean best cause it's fun. I could see some fish in the water. We saw banana trees and ate lots of pineapple. We went on a boat at Pearl Harbor.

I'm in first grade now. My teacher is Mrs. Shaw. I am learning adding and spelling and reading. I like recess best. I like to eat in the cafeteria.

Bradley and Nathan going snorkeling in Hawaii, 1988

Chapter 9

A WINNING ATTITUDE

Soon after we moved to Utah, Kristi joined The Sunshine Generation, a singing and dancing group, with some of her new friends. Dressed in bright, sunshine-like colors, they performed at rest homes and elementary schools. Since they also got to do cool things like march in parades and perform at Lagoon amusement park, Brad decided to give it a try. Actually, it took some convincing to get him to launch a singing career. We felt it was important for him to have some interests besides sports, since his health could interfere with his ability to compete athletically. Even as a six-year-old he felt that it wasn't very macho to sing and dance on stage, but the fringe benefits outweighed the potential for embarrassment. He was in first grade, and completely bald. In his age group there were about ten girls and one other boy besides Brad.

Brad's uniform consisted of white pants (which were too tight in the waist when he was on steroids), a yellow shirt, and an orange vest. A white cowboy hat completed the ensemble. He stuck it out as a Sunshine Boy for the school year, but that was all. He wanted to be an athlete. He was much happier on the soccer field than in dance class.

When it came to sports, Brad was a legend in his own mind. He started playing soccer in recreational leagues when he was five and sometimes even kicked the ball in the right direction. He never seemed to notice that he wasn't a very good player. He believed so strongly in his athletic skills that the facts did little to alter his opinion of his abilities. Fortunately, the other players and coaches were kind and allowed him to play, congratulating him on every tiny success. He continued to play on soccer teams until he was in sixth grade. By that time all the boys his age had either given up soccer or were playing on serious competitive teams.

During his last season of play, our neighbor, Lynn Van Leeuwen, the father of Brad's friend Ricky, coached him. They had a winning team, with lots of talented players being recruited by competition teams. Brad played all season, kicking the ball occasionally, and cheering enthusiastically from the sidelines when he was not on the field.

At the end of the final game of the season, Brad's team led their opponents by several points. Coach Van Leeuwen discreetly asked the other boys to set up Brad so he could score a goal. They tried their best. Brad was given several good passes within easy range of the goal. He swung and missed at some, others fell short of the goal or went the wrong way. Even the opposing team seemed willing to help, giving him the opportunity to kick and waiting to see where the ball would go. If it had come close to the goal, I think the goalie would have stepped back and watched it roll in.

Since this was real life and not a movie script, that never happened. He didn't score, in spite of everyone's best efforts. To the credit of the coach and the other boys, no one said anything negative to him. He was part of the team---one of the winners---even if his main contribution was to yell loudly from the sidelines.

Brad participated in as many sports as he could. He took ice skating lessons when he was five. He learned to ski and even got the chance to try out his dream sport, snowboarding. When our family got together for wally-ball games, he was as competitive as anyone.

Because he was short and not very speedy, basketball was a particularly challenging sport for Brad, but one he loved. Thurl Bailey, a well-known player on the Salt Lake Jazz professional basketball team, sponsored a basketball camp every summer. The kids associated with Make-A-Wish Foundation were invited to participate free of charge. Brad attended the camp for three summers. Mr. Bailey emphasized sportsmanship and personal improvement as much as winning. Brad loved those camps. He spent hours after school in our neighbor's driveway, dribbling the ball and shooting time after time. In 1993 when Salt Lake had record snowfalls, Brad was thrilled to be able to make slam dunks, standing on snow piled six feet high.

In the Young Men's program at church, Brad played the most competitive basketball of his life. He was four-feet-ten-inches tall, about a foot shorter than the majority of other boys his age. He sat in the folding chairs on the sidelines, begging the coach to put him in. I sat on the opposite side of the room, silently begging the coach not to let Brad play. Brad knew the mechanics of the game. He knew if he could just get his legs to move fast, get the ball to dribble in control, and then make the perfect shot, he could win the game. His head knew what his body should do, what Brad could picture himself doing, even if reality painted a different picture. But it was the picture he carried of himself: a winner, the best, capable of anything, and immune to discouragement.

Brad waiting for a ride on the kneeboard at Folsom Lake, California, August 1990

Brad in his soccer uniform, 1992

Chapter 10

RADIATION THERAPY

Brad had lost his hair again during the summer of 1988 as a result of reinduction chemotherapy. He started first grade with a little stubble growing back. It looked almost like the short summer buzz cuts that a lot of other little boys had. He asked me to get approval for him to wear a hat at school, mainly because he thought wearing hats was cool, but also because he would go bald again when he started radiation treatment in a few months. The school had a strict policy against hats of any kind, but he was given permission to wear one because of his medical condition.

Since Brad had to stay at school a full day in first grade, it was important for him to go to bed early every night so he would have the energy to get through the school day. By evening he was tired, and willing to go right to bed. Brad was always interested in getting his "beauty sleep." Sometimes he would even disappear during the afternoon, and after anxiously searching the neighborhood, I would find him sound asleep in his bed.

On hospital days, Brad usually attended an hour or two of school before I picked him up for his appointment so he would not miss any more class time than necessary. After our four or five hours at the clinic, he often fell asleep on the way home if he wasn't throwing up. IV chemotherapy produced nausea in nearly every child. Anyone who was trailing an IV pole also had a "barf bucket" issued as standard equipment. We always had one with us in the car for the trip home. It typically took a few hours for Brad's stomach to settle after chemotherapy. Occasionally, the nausea lasted all night and into the next day. But more often than not, after he rested a bit he was ready to resume normal activities and put the treatments out of his mind until the next appointment.

Bradley's protocol after his central nervous system relapse included a round of radiation therapy during December 1988. The radiation treatments were done at LDS Hospital, down the hill from Primary Children's. In the waiting room everyone, in addition to being a cancer patient, was old. Old people with canes, walkers, and worried faces filled the seats. During our daily visits there they got to know Brad, who became a spark of sunshine in their day. He was not at all concerned about the radiation, having been assured that it did not involve any "pokes" and was just like getting an x-ray.

At his first appointment he was measured, and black X's were drawn with permanent ink onto his bald head and down his spine. They served as a target so the radiation would hit exactly the right areas of his body and hopefully avoid unnecessary damage to vital organs. Brad hid the X's on his head with his red, white, and blue bicycle hat. He received daily radiation for about three weeks.

Brad was a favorite of the staff in radiology. They felt sad that such a small boy had to go through cancer treatment, but he was a wonderful break from the very sick old people they were used to treating. He finished the series of radiation shortly before Christmas. On the last day of his treatment, someone had arranged for Santa Claus to visit the clinic. Since Brad was the only child there, he had his pick of toys and was loaded up with several items to take home and share with his siblings.

During the previous summer Dave and I felt that another child would be a welcome addition to our family.

Five days after Brad's seventh birthday, our baby, Shane, was born. Our children were excited to have a new baby brother.

Going to the clinic at the hospital became as much a part of Shane's life as it was Brad's. For Shane it was a fun outing. Occasionally during the summers he stayed home with the older kids, but most of the time he went with Bradley and me on "doctor days." The same volunteer "Grandma" was at the clinic every Wednesday, our usual appointment day, and always made Shane feel like she had just been waiting for him to come. Shane liked to sit at the craft table and do projects with her. As active as he was, he learned to be careful of IV lines.

Shane was hard to keep up with when he started to walk. One day a volunteer was watching him in the playroom while I went to the treatment room with Brad for his spinal tap. I heard an announcement over the speaker saying a little boy had been found in the radiology lab. From the description I realized it was Shane. He had escaped from the playroom and was probably trying to find the cafeteria and the soft pretzels that we often got for a treat. From that point on I kept him with Brad and me while we were at the hospital.

When Shane was old enough to start school, he was quite indignant to think that Brad got to go to the hospital without him. He wanted us to wait until after school so he could come. Since chemo days required a minimum of four hours at the hospital that was not an option.

Construction of the new, badly needed, Primary Children's Hospital was completed in February 1990. We were invited to take a tour during the open house. The new building was a huge improvement over the old facility. All the patient rooms were private and spacious, with a private bathroom and a foldout cot for parents. The waiting room was large and colorful. Tanks of tropical fish and children's artwork added to the pleasant atmosphere. As much as we liked the new building, we hoped that we would never need to spend the night there. Brad was nearing the end of his second series of treatment, staying in remission and feeling great. We were anxious to end our regular visits to the hospital and have him off treatment and cancer free.

Brad's Journal Entry, January 7, 1990

I am in second grade now. I've been there for at least two years. My teacher is Miss Taysom. She is nice. I am learning about clocks.

At Thanksgiving we went to Grandma Coles' house. We saw our cousins and aunts and uncles there. We went to Disneyland. I liked the cars when I drove my Dad crazy, and the haunted house.

For Christmas I got a hyper-driver car and a race car set, and a stuffed monkey, a fanny pack, and Legos, and games and a Nintendo and clothes. During vacation we went swimming inside and bowling and to a show. Yesterday we went to a frozen lake and saw people ice fishing. My sister was afraid to go on the ice.

Chapter 11

A BREAK FROM CHEMO

While in second grade Brad began to show signs of learning problems. He worked hard and was conscientious about finishing assignments, even ones he missed while he was at the hospital. He was reading at about grade level and keeping up with math, but he had difficulty retaining in memory the things he learned. Spelling was a particular challenge for him. He brought home his list of words on Monday. I helped him study every day, and by Friday he spelled them all correctly on the spelling test. As soon as the test was done, he forgot them all. Instead of his reading ability improving, he began struggling with comprehension and word recognition. Miss Taysom worked with him, and he finished the school year with a passing report card.

Each new milestone in Brad's life caused me to reflect on the blessing that he was still alive. Rather than just assume experiences would automatically follow one after the next, I wondered: would he live to be three, to loose a baby tooth, to go to school? Each time he arrived at another significant event, I gave thanks that he was still with us. When he turned eight years old in April 1990, he reached such a milestone. He was ready to be baptized. I was grateful that he was not just alive, but doing so well.

Brad's baptismal service was held on May 5 at our church building. Our Bishop, Max Oldroyd, gave a talk during the service. He said that Brad was a very special person with an important mission to perform in life. Dave performed the baptism, then confirmed Brad a member of the church and gave him the gift of the Holy Ghost. During the blessing Brad was told that the disease would leave his body and that he would be healthy.

It might seem that Brad did not receive that promised blessing. He was not cured. However, from the time of that blessing he enjoyed good health for more than a year. He was completely off chemotherapy treatment for nine months, the last time in his life that he would be free from taking drugs.

Brad's prospects for third grade seemed promising. His last chemotherapy was finished in October, so he would not need to miss school for weekly trips to the hospital. However, right from the start of the year it was evident that he was falling farther behind his classmates. His teacher, Mrs. Enger, felt he could benefit from being in the resource program, where children are sent to receive specialized attention for learning problems. I worried about his self-esteem. Having cancer already made him different. I didn't want him to feel he was "dumb" as well. Mrs. Enger explained that most of the class would not even know he was going to resource, since students left the class for all sorts of programs during the day. I met with the resource teacher, and we decided to try putting Brad in her class for a few hours a week. He took a test to see if he qualified for special help. Though academically he did not, his medical problems made him eligible.

Brad liked going to resource. He liked the change in his day, the teacher, and the additional help. He felt successful in that setting. He remained involved in the resource program for a small part of each school day through elementary and middle school and was able to stay up well enough with his classmates to advance every year to the next grade. Holding him back would not have helped him anyway, since he was doing the best he could. He studied hard, always turned in assignments, and kept up as well as he was able.

I felt sure the learning problems he experienced were a result of the effects of radiation to his head, in combination with the cancer in his central nervous system and the chemotherapy he received at a time when his body should have been growing rapidly. He could learn most things, but at a much slower rate than normal. He struggled with short-term memory. The doctors told me there was no medical research to substantiate my feelings. However, the problems did not start until after he had received radiation. A friend, whose son had received radiation for a brain tumor, described to me her son's similar learning difficulties.

WAYS TO GET A'S IN CLASS By Brad Coles November 4, 1998

1. *Bring in your homework*
2. *Be on time for class*
3. *Don't miss any days of class*
4. *Don't talk*
5. *Do well on homework and tests*
6. *Do extra credit*
7. *Get plenty of sleep each night*
8. *Ask good questions*
9. *Make good notes*
10. *Don't be saying things you shouldn't*
11. *Make good use of time in class*
12. *Do as you are told*

Pie eating contest at Camp Hobe, June 1996 (Brad is seated second from right with his face in a pie)

Chapter 12

CAMP HOBE

The local unit of the American Cancer Society sponsors a camp each summer for childhood cancer patients and their siblings. It was Rachel, the child life worker, who introduced us to Camp Hobe. In addition to working with children in the oncology clinic, Rachel was the camp director, known as "Mother Nature." She told Brad how much fun camp was and encouraged him to attend. He was only seven, and I thought he was too young to stay at a four-day-long camp, but he thought otherwise. Since his older siblings could go with him, Dave and I decided a little hesitantly to let them participate.

Having Brad away from us for even a few days made us nervous. We realized that each day apart was one less we could share with him. But the reason we were keeping him alive was so that he could enjoy living. It was a dilemma we faced every time he wanted to do something risky, since we worked so hard to keep him alive. Camp was hardly dangerous, but I was not used to letting anyone else be responsible for Brad's care, even if they were oncology medical professionals. It turned out that participating in Camp Hobe was one of the highlights of his life and the source of some of the most special memories our other children have of their brother.

The location for Camp Hobe was in the mountains about an hour and a half drive from home. I dropped the kids off there on a Wednesday morning, and Dave and I picked them up the following Saturday. If the term

"Happy Camper" has ever been used appropriately, it would describe the kids at the end of Camp Hobe. A few kids were on crutches, many were bald, some were pale and thin, others puffy cheeked. But they were all having the time of their lives.

Our excited children all talked at once on the drive home, telling of their adventures and new friends. We learned all about the chubby bunny game. There had been doorbell ditching and water balloon fights. A counselor's underwear had flown from the flagpole. They had enjoyed crafts, campfires, and hikes, as with any camp. But most importantly for these kids, there was a bond of being in a special club. They knew what the others were going through. No one had to explain needle marks, IV lines, catheters, or baldness. They were a bunch of kids like kids everywhere, but with a deeper understanding of the importance of making the most of every fun moment.

The camp staff members, in addition to Mother Nature, were known by names such as "Captain Ron," "Dances With Squirrels," and "Lieutenant Dan." They threw dignity to the wind and let the kids have fun with them, often at the expense of their own pride. Many of Brad's closest friends were those he made over the years at camp.

After the first year at camp, it was never a question again of whether the kids wanted to go back. Brad started asking about the registration forms in about January every year. All of our kids loved their camp experiences. Nathan and Janene both volunteered as junior counselors at camp for several years.

Janene's Memories of Camp Hobe, 1999

I have more stories about Camp Hobe than I could ever write down, so I will tell some that are the most vivid in my mind, the stories that I will never forget.

Every year we had a pie eating contest and every year Brad had to enter. It was absolutely hilarious to see him with his entire face covered in pie, trying to keep up with the big boys. He never won, but that didn't bother him. Just as long as he got a little pie on his face he was happy. I think he also liked it because he was in a good position to start a pie-throwing contest. Now that, I do believe he won!

Brad loved "Hobe Jam." They had a band come to camp and play music for us to dance to. I thought it was so fun to watch Brad up there jumping around to the music. If you asked him he would tell you that he started Hobe Jam. He was such a funny kid!

Early on in our Camp Hobe experiences, I think it was about '92 or '93, some of the camp leaders got really daring and actually shaved their heads! That's right, shaved their heads bald. It was my counselor, Julie, who started the trend. It was originally part of a skit, and she was supposed to pretend, but in the end she decided that she really wanted to shave it. Before the skit we shaved her head and put a towel over it to hide the damage. Then during the skit, we took the towel off her head to reveal what we had done. Everyone just about died. I couldn't believe how excited the bald kids were. I think just seeing how happy it made the kids convinced two of the other leaders, Mother Nature and Irish, to shave their heads too. The kids loved it! The counselors at camp are really loving and sympathetic.

Something that Brad always loved at camp was "I am a Chubby Bunny." The object of Chubby Bunny is to cram as many marshmallows in your mouth at a time as possible and still be able to say, "I am a chubby bunny." It was hilarious to watch. Brad loved to sit on the front row and cheer on his favorite counselor. I think the record, when I was last at camp, was thirty-four marshmallows! Oh yeah, the best part about winning the Chubby Bunny contest was the prize . . . a bag of marshmallows! Yuck!

One thing that I think Brad will be remembered for at camp is the Spam. Technically it was Nathan that started the Spam sacrifice, but Brad was behind the idea one hundred per cent. Nathan was the Spam Man and Brad was Spam Man Junior, or Spam Man II. Every year we had a Spam sacrifice where we actually set a tin of Spam on our campfire and cooked it. Then we passed it around and everyone who was daring enough took a bite of it. Nathan and Brad always had to be the first to take a bite. To this day they still do the Spam sacrifice at camp. Shane, Spam Man III, has been able to carry on this tradition since Brad hasn't been here to do it and Nathan was away on his mission.

Nathan's Application to be a Camp Hobe Counselor, 1999

I would like to be a Junior Counselor for many reasons, among which are both serious and less serious reasons. I believe I have something to offer the kids that is quite rare in a person my age. Not only will I enjoy playing with the kids, but I will enjoy somber moments as well. I really enjoy laughing with the kids, but I also enjoy crying with them when it is appropriate. I also think many of the kids are looking for a good big brother (who sometimes dresses like their sister) to look out for them and show each one of them that he cares. I know from personal experience as a camper that it is scary to feel alone. That is why the junior counselors can often reach the children on a level that is missed by the senior counselors.

I enjoy a good water fight.

I know the official term we run under is Counselors in Training and I believe this concept to be extremely beneficial. I think the junior counselor should not feel their responsibilities as less necessary than that of the seniors, but rather that they are just as responsible for what they are given jurisdiction over as is the senior counselor. It is a privilege for me to serve as a Counselor in Training under a wonderful and talented counselor because great lessons can be learned, both by the J.C. and the counselors.

I only get to dress in "Drag" once a year, and boy, do I look ravishing!

Not only do we counselors benefit, the kids greatly benefit. They are given personalized attention that could otherwise not be met by the counselors. I remember this lesson to be especially poignant as I took care of little Jason, who was blind, and wondered how a counselor could devote such time to a single individual. We as Counselors in Training optimize and further camp. We are the junior counselors who make Camp Hobe the best place beneath the sun.

We also are the Junior Counselors who make SPAM the best food beneath the sun.

I would love to once again be a part of this wonderful organization. It is the least I can give back after all of the wonderful memories that camp has offered me. I would also like to dedicate this year's service to my little brother, Brad, who recently passed away from leukemia. I know that as I help out the kids around the camp, I will feel the laughter that Brad would have expressed if he were around to share it. I would like to share this laughter for Brad with these wonderful kids through my service as a Counselor in

Training. If you would please consider this and then give me the chance, I would appreciate it. Thank you. Nate Coles

Brad at Camp Hobe, 1996

Chapter 13

REMAINING OPTIMISTIC

In July of 1991, four of our children went to Camp Hobe. That was the maximum number of kids allowed per family that year since the camp had limited space. Shane was only two and not old enough to go, and Alisa stayed home to get a job, as she had just turned sixteen. Arriving at camp, the kids grabbed their belongings to take to their cabins. Searching hurriedly under the seats and in the back of the van, Nathan asked in dismay, "Where is my red duffel bag?"

"Did you put it in the car?" I asked.

He obviously had not. The carefully selected items of clothing and toiletries were still at home. There seemed to be no choice but for us to drive one and a half hours each way and retrieve his forgotten bag. He had a coat and sleeping bag with him, but nothing else. The counselors assured us there were plenty of extra clothes in the lost and found. Just to be sure he had something to wear, Dave and I drove to the nearest town and bought him a sweat suit, swim trunks, underwear, socks, and a toothbrush. It was probably a wasted effort since he never changed clothes the whole time anyway, but we felt better knowing he at least had the option. That year he won the coveted "dirtiest camper" award.

After a few quiet days at home with just Alisa and Shane, it was time to pick up the others from camp. We went prepared with swimming suits and inner tubes so we could float down the small river near the camp entrance before returning home.

Brad was excited to share his stories of the adventures of camp, as were the other kids. He and Janene laughed as they told us that Brad had been visiting in her cabin, playing around on her bed, when he fell off and went under the fabric wall of the cabin, landing outside. He seemed healthy and full of energy. It had been nine months since he had completed the second series of chemotherapy and radiation. We thought this was the last year of camp for our kids, since they were eligible to go for only one year after finishing treatment.

The kids performed their camp skits, sang songs, and collected addresses and phone numbers of fellow campers before saying good-bye. Our family went over to the river to go tubing together. We put on our swimsuits and felt the icy water, almost changing our minds about floating, but the hot day made the water bearable. When I saw Brad with only his swim trunks on, I was alarmed by the number of bruises he had. They were mostly small, but they were all over his body. He and Janene thought it was because he had played roughly, including the fall out of the cabin. That could account for some of them, but I was really worried about the number of them and the fact that they were in places where bruises are unusual, like on his chest and back.

Dave thought I was being paranoid when I told him I was concerned about a relapse. He felt that Brad was just showing the battle scars of a week of good fun. But I could feel it: the oppressive fear and inescapable knowledge that the leukemia was back, that it was probably never gone, that Brad would be subjected to more pain and testing, and that his chances of survival had just dropped through the floor. I knew all that before we took him to the emergency room the next day. He wasn't acting sick, but the doctor agreed that a large number of bruises was cause for concern.

Dr. Arness was there to give us the bad news. I was prepared to be nicer to her than I had been to Dr. Short when we learned of Brad's first relapse. That time I had blamed him for the relapse, even though I knew it was not his fault. When Dr. Arness came in with “the look,” grim faced and serious, I reminded myself to stay under control. I still was hurt, devastated, deeply sad, but I didn’t blame her. For a long time I didn’t like her, but I didn’t blame her.

The relapse was in Brad’s bone marrow, not the central nervous system as the first relapse had been. Bone marrow relapses are more serious and do not respond as well to treatment. Statistically, his chance of long-term survival was less than 25 percent, probably much less, but we tried to remain optimistic. Brad was disappointed by the diagnosis, but not defeated. One of his first observations was, “Well, at least I still get to go to camp next year.” He was sure he would beat the leukemia.

At this point, there was not a standard protocol to follow, but the doctors felt the first thing to do was a round of reinduction chemotherapy in heavy doses to try and get Brad into remission again. If that worked, they wanted us to start thinking about a bone marrow transplant. Two weeks later leukemia cells were found in his testicles. It seemed that things were going from bad to worse.

One positive thing we found was that some advancements had been made in comfort measures since his previous round of treatment. The most exciting finding was a new drug, which controlled the nausea that resulted from chemotherapy. Brad started taking one of the new anti-nausea pills before receiving an IV drip, and “barf buckets” became a thing of the past. The first time he tried the pill I could not believe it would actually work, but it did. It was just too amazing.

Brad started fourth grade about two months after the diagnosis of relapse. He was still in the reinduction phase of treatment and was going to be missing a lot of school time for chemotherapy and more radiation. His teacher was Mrs. Moss, and he loved her, as did all the kids in the school. She made sure the students in her class were all friends to each other, and especially to Brad, who had come back to school bald that year. They were all like miniature bodyguards to him. If someone in the halls that didn't know about his medical problems said something hurtful about his baldness, Brad's classmates stood up to the offender and explained that he had cancer.

One evening shortly after the start of the school year while Dave was out of town on business, I was preparing dinner. Some of the kids were doing homework and Brad was playing a Nintendo game. Janene came downstairs to play also, and when she walked into the family room, she suddenly started to scream, "Mom, Mom! Something is wrong with Brad!"

I dropped what I was doing and rushed to where Brad had fallen on the floor and was convulsing from head to toe. I had never seen anyone have a seizure before, but there was no question what was happening. Trying to stay calm, I asked Janene to go call the hospital. She said she didn't know how, so I ran to get the phone myself, instructing Alisa to sit with Brad. We did not have a cordless phone, so I had to stand in the dining area of the kitchen to make the call. Beth, one of Brad's nurses at the clinic answered, and I explained that Brad was having a seizure. Very calmly, she said, "I want you to hang up now and dial 9-1-1."

The 9-1-1 dispatcher remained on the phone with me to monitor Brad's condition as we waited for paramedics to arrive. Gradually Brad's convulsions had subsided, but he was still not conscious. The sirens of the ambulance brought the entire neighborhood to our front yard. Realizing I would have to go with Brad in the ambulance, I called Kristi, who was at her friend Tammy's house, to come home and help out. There were plenty of neighbors standing around wondering what they should do. Larry Jensen ran over from across the street and offered to give Brad a priesthood blessing. One of the paramedics, who was also a priesthood holder in the LDS church, volunteered to assist in the blessing. They offered the prayer for Bradley as he was lying on a gurney in our front entry, ready for the ride to the hospital. As always, the blessing brought me comfort and the peaceful knowledge that Brad was in the hands of the Lord.

Rachel Roatcap, the mother of Brad's best friend Jonathan, happened to be driving up the street when all the excitement occurred. She was on her way home from work, going to take care of her own family, but when she learned about Brad's seizure she insisted on going to the hospital with me. She followed the ambulance in her car and met us at the emergency room. Her presence was reassuring to Brad as well as to me.

Brad was tired, but fully alert by the time we reached the hospital. He was confused by what had happened. The doctor on call recommended we spend the night at the hospital so they could observe Brad and conduct tests to determine the cause of the seizure. It seemed clear to me that it was related to his latest relapse and the continued chemotherapy. After all the scans and tests were completed, the only thing we knew was that his brain showed signs of having a seizure.

We visited with a neurologist who put Brad on a medication to control seizures. Just what he needed---more pills. After a night at the hospital he seemed to be doing fine, so we went home, and he went back to school with one more thing to worry about.

Chapter 14

ROYAL TREATMENT

Soon after Brad relapsed for the second time, we contacted the Make-A-Wish Foundation about granting him the wish of his dreams, as they do for thousands of critically ill children. Although Brad had been eligible to receive a wish after his first relapse we did not pursue it at that time. We still hoped he would be cured. Turning to Make-A-Wish now was like admitting openly that he might not survive.

The only limitation to what kids can ask is that the wish be their very own, not influenced by parents, siblings, or anyone else. Choosing a wish was agonizingly difficult for Brad. He knew lots of children that had received wishes. Many of their ideas sounded tempting to him. He thought a daylong shopping spree at a toy store would be pretty amazing. He also considered asking for a camping trailer or a cruise. The older kids in the family kept telling him how fun it would be to go to Walt Disney World.

Two Wish Granters came to our home to talk to Brad about his wish. First they talked with the whole family, but when it came time to discuss the actual wish, the rest of the family was invited to leave the room so that the decision would be Brad's alone. We all wondered what he would choose. It was almost like having a magic genie in a bottle come and grant any wish in the whole world. We didn't want him to blow it.

Soon we were asked back into the room, and the Wish Granters announced that Brad had chosen to go to

Disney World. I still wonder if that was his personal first choice, or the one he knew would make his sisters and brothers happy. He had a very caring nature. Whatever his reasons, no one was disappointed. We chose the first week of November for our trip, since Make-A-Wish needed a few weeks to arrange tickets and accommodations. The whole family, all eight of us, would be going.

We started making plans for our trip. Everyone was so excited to be going, amazed by the gift of a completely free vacation. The more details we learned from Make-A-Wish, the more we were in awe of this incredibly generous organization. There is a whole resort near Disney World called "Kids' Village," built expressly for the families of children on trips from Make-A-Wish or similar organizations worldwide. It had not always been possible to find suitable accommodations for children receiving wishes at the needed time and some passed away before their wish could be granted. Kids Village was built so there would never be another child denied a wish because there was no place to stay.

In early October, just as all the plans for Brad's wish trip were being finalized, Brad went to the hospital for a regular chemotherapy infusion. When his blood counts came back, we were hit with an unexpected bombshell. Even though Brad seemed well, there were blast cells in his blood. He was nearly through with the reinduction phase of his third round of chemotherapy. The high doses of drugs he was receiving should have put him into remission. It was devastating news. Brad's first thoughts were about his trip. Maybe the doctors would not let him go. Maybe he would be too sick to have fun.

I talked in private to a doctor about postponing the trip. His immediate response was, "Go now. The sooner the better." With another relapse occurring only weeks after the previous one, even while on high dose chemotherapy, it appeared the leukemia was not responding to the drugs this time. Brad's life was in danger. I was afraid to ask the doctor for a time frame of how much longer he might live, and he was reluctant to offer one.

Finally I said, "Are we looking at weeks or months?"

The response, "Probably weeks, and not very many."

As soon as he learned we were still going to take the trip, Brad was as happy as ever. Somehow he had the ability to put aside all the negative aspects of his life and live for the positive things. He must have had unseen help from angels. I also felt encouraged that things were going to work out all right. I might have been in denial, but it seemed impossible that Brad was only weeks away from the end of his life. His energy was limited because of the drugs and disease, but his enthusiasm was boundless. We were going to Disney World!

The night before our trip, Brad's friend, Brad Crawford, came to our house and handed Dave an envelope containing a huge amount of money. There was a strong bond between our son and the adult friend that shared his name. Dave asked why he was giving us the money, and he replied that it was to help make sure we did all the fun things we wanted on our trip. The only stipulation was that we were to spend every penny of it before we came back. We never learned if anyone else contributed to the money Brad gave us, or if he donated the whole amount himself. That act of generosity went on our long list of amazing gifts we experienced that week. We did spend every penny and had a great time doing it.

The day we boarded the plane for Orlando, we had no idea how the week would turn out. We didn't know if Brad would be healthy enough to enjoy the trip, if he would need to rest a lot, or even if he would come back alive. But we were happy and excited to be going, determined to make the most of every minute and carve the memories into our hearts.

Make-A-Wish had arranged for us to stay at the Walt Disney World Yacht Club Resort. The Kids' Village had cottages for most wish children and their families, but they accommodated only six people and we had eight. We felt we got the best possible combination of room and meal arrangements. Our two adjoining rooms at the resort were luxurious beyond anything we were used to in our family travels. The kids were thrilled to find there were even phones in the bathrooms! There were swimming pools, hot tubs, and access to the lagoon from a dock behind the hotel. The excitement affected even two-year-old Shane. Our first morning in the hotel, he stood up in his crib and yelled, "Nathan, Nathan, wake up! We're going to Forida!"

For meals we went to the Kids' Village and ate in the Gingerbread Cottage, where there are peppermint candies laminated into the surface of all the tables. Our first morning there we were delighted to find LDS missionaries serving our breakfast as part of their community service. Disney characters visited personally with the kids and posed for pictures. Employees from Gatorland park brought in live alligators. The kids were given toys to take home. Brad received a giant green stuffed Ninja Turtle, a character from one of his favorite cartoon shows at that time. We joked that we would have to reserve another seat on the airplane to get it home. The badge that Brad wore said, "Give Kids the World." He pinned it to his new florescent green Disney World hat, and it identified him to the staff as a Wish Kid, which meant royal treatment.

Brad rode in a wheelchair because he did not have the strength to walk long distances through the park, and we wanted to see everything. We had a handicapped sticker to hang in our rental van so close parking was always available. The van might have been the only disappointment of the trip from our children's perspective.

It was similar to the one we owned, except it was blue instead of red, and held fifteen passengers, while ours held twelve. It was the only rental vehicle large enough for our family.

The wheelchair Brad used gave us access to the front of all the lines, and Brad's "Give Kids the World" pin let him be first to greet characters. He was thrilled when he got to meet the Teenage Mutant Ninja Turtle characters and have his picture taken with them. Kristi's fifteenth birthday was the day we were at Epcot Center. We celebrated by having lunch there at a German restaurant. For dessert they brought her a whole cake decorated with a Mickey Mouse. It was our favorite part of the meal.

One of the gifts on his Wish Trip was a family meal at the Hard Rock Cafe. All of us except Brad chose a mid-priced entree. Brad ordered steak. There was nothing Brad loved eating more than a big, juicy steak. It was a real treat for him. When his meal arrived, the steak was huge, as was the smile on his face when he saw it. He ate every bite, then topped it off with a banana split. It was hard to imagine this kid could be in his final weeks of life.

Whenever we ate out that week, the kids ordered anything they wanted without concern about the cost. They were each able to buy some special things to take home. The entire time we felt in awe of the generosity of complete strangers, as well as our good friends at home, which allowed us to have such a wonderful time. We definitely felt that our whole family, not just Brad, had been given the world.

Throughout the trip, Brad stayed healthy. We explored every part of Disney World and Universal Studios. At a dinner theater called "King Henry's Feast," Nathan was selected as our table's server. One day we visited the Kennedy Space Center, then walked on Cocoa Beach where a man gave Shane a conch shell he had found. We took tons of pictures to remind us of the incredible experience of Brad's Make-A-Wish trip.

Brad continued his treatment after our return home. Although he had given me his Christmas wish list weeks earlier, as had the other children, he didn't know that I had not yet bought any gifts for him. The doctor's words from the day he had his third relapse were too real in my mind. But Brad did not appear to be dying. In fact, he felt great. He was in school every day that he did not have to go to the hospital and had energy to play with friends. Finally I went Christmas shopping for him, which was a good thing, since he was alive and well at Christmas time.

Brad's Journal Entry, January 1992

I am right now nine years old. I will turn ten in April and get a ten-speed (bike). I have a girl friend too. Her name is Katie. I am in fourth grade and in my class we got a new kid. My teacher's name is Mrs. Moss. She's a nice lady. Today I am going to the hospital. I have to have a drip. We got our basement done.

As Brad completed the reinduction phase of chemotherapy, it was time to decide what to do next. In spite of predictions to the contrary, he had gone into remission yet again. However, in our discussions of further treatment options, none seemed very promising. We decided to pursue the possibility of a bone marrow transplant. Because Brad had five siblings, the odds of one of them being a perfect match to be a donor were very high. Statistically, there is a one in four chance that a sibling will match 100 percent.

After the whole family was tested, we were disappointed that no one was even close to a perfect match. The only one who would be considered as a donor was Dave, who matched on four of six components. There was still a possibility of finding a match through a donor bank, which at that time would have been a long shot. Searching for a match was an expensive process, not covered by insurance, very time consuming, with no guarantee of a match. In order for Brad to have a transplant he would have to go to Seattle or Los Angeles, the nearest locations where pediatric bone marrow transplants were being performed. He would stay a minimum of six months, maybe longer if there were serious complications. He might not survive the transplant procedure, which required intensive chemotherapy and full body radiation. Even if the transplant was a success, there were complications to deal with afterwards. A relapse could still occur, even after transplant. It was not a pretty picture.

Dave and I did research on transplants, prayed and fasted about what to do. Neither of us felt comfortable with him receiving a transplant. We did not feel good about Brad and me leaving the rest of the family for six months or more for an experimental procedure that might actually shorten his life rather than cure him. Brad was involved in the decision making to an extent, but as he was only nine years old, the choice was really up to us as his parents. We opted to try another round of chemotherapy. No matter which treatment we chose his chance for survival was slim.

This was a very spiritually challenging time for Dave and me. We felt that we needed guidance from the Lord in deciding how to care for Brad, and yet little inspiration was coming. One evening we went to the Jordan River Temple, hoping to find some answers to our concerns about making the best choices for Brad's care. During our time there, we both came to the same conclusion: Brad's life was in the Lord's hands. We did not need to bear the burden of whether he lived or died. The scripture came to Dave's mind, "Be still, and know that I am God." From that point we were both at peace that whatever happened in Brad's life would be the will of the Lord. I felt like the burden of worry over what was right for him was physically lifted off my shoulders. We did not have to be responsible for the outcome of his life, only for providing the best care we could for whatever length of time he was alive.

Once it appeared that Brad was going to live, at least for a while, he was told he needed to have a permanent catheter placed in his chest to receive his medication. Most patients were now having the catheters implanted as soon as they were diagnosed, but since Brad had started treatment years earlier, he had never gotten nor wanted one. Other than on two occasions when a "pic line" had been inserted into his arm to give long-term access for repeated IV's, all of his chemo drips had been given through his favorite veins in his elbow joint. Those veins could still be used to draw blood, but the nurses were adamant about a permanent line. It was no longer a choice of whether to get one. His veins would not withstand much more chemo. The only choice was which type of line to have implanted.

Two types of catheters were available: a Broviac and a Port-A-Cath. The Broviac, which was preferred by the doctors, was implanted under the skin of the chest, attached to a large vein, which enabled the chemo to be distributed quickly throughout the body. A piece of plastic tubing a few inches long protruded through the skin, allowing instant access for IV's without a "poke." The site around the tubing had to be cleaned carefully each day, and the line flushed with heparin to keep it from clotting shut.

The Port-A-Cath was similar in its function. The main difference was it was placed completely under the skin with no exposed tubing. Other than a slight bulge on the chest it was not visible and it required no daily care. He could swim, shower, or take his shirt off to play ball and not have a tube hanging out of his chest. The disadvantage was a needle stick was still required to access the catheter. Brad was not particularly concerned about needles, unless they were in his back, and was sure from the beginning of our discussions that the Port-A-Cath was the only option he would consider. We looked at dolls with both types of lines and talked to other patients about their personal choices, but Brad was not willing to have anything so visible as the Broviac line. The Port-A-Cath was his choice.

Surgery to implant the catheter was minor but required general anesthesia. Dave and I took Brad to the outpatient surgery unit early in the morning of his scheduled procedure. Only months before he had gone there for the biopsy of his testicles. He once again chose bubble-gum-scented gas and was wheeled away for the surgery. We waited anxiously in the room with other nervous parents. The procedure went well, and we rejoined him a short time later in the recovery room. The catheter was in place and two small incisions were visible on his chest and neck.

The scars from that surgery were more physical evidence of the invisible battle going on in his small body between the healthy and diseased cells. When we went swimming, I would look at the physical scars of his treatment and wonder if anyone else noticed them. It was amazing that he could be so sick, but appear so healthy. In addition to the scars and bulge on his chest from the Port-A-Cath, the skin over the vertebra in the small of his back was pock marked and dented from numerous spinal taps. His right hip, at the dimple, was similarly scarred and permanently bruised from bone marrow aspirations.

Our family with some of the characters at Disney World, November 1991 (Back row left to right: Diane holding Shane, Nathan next to Pluto, Janene, Alisa, Mickey, Dave; Front row: Brad between the Chipmunks, Kristi, and Snow White)

Chapter 15

CHILD LIFE BUDDIES

Among the professionals who work with the kids at Primary Children's Hospital are the child life specialists, basically a cross between trained social workers, camp counselors, and good friends. They play games with the kids and sit through painful procedures, helping to provide distractions and comforts. Rachel was the first child life specialist to work in the oncology clinic during the time we were there. She was an uninhibited free spirit, and the kids loved her. In addition to her duties in the clinic, she was the director of Camp Hobe, where she was affectionately known as "Mother Nature."

Rachel was a great friend to Brad, and he was saddened when he heard of her plans to move to California. The clinic and camp would not be the same without her. Brad felt a little better about Rachel leaving, though, when he learned that Amy was going to be the new child life specialist. She was a recent college graduate from Alabama, with a soft Southern accent. She made Brad feel like he was her best friend. Maybe all the other kids felt the same connection to her. She talked to him about school, his friends, his concerns. She played games with him and made sure he got special prizes to take home. Instead of giving him a single package of baseball cards after procedures, she gave him whole boxes full. Brad always went to find Amy as soon as we got to the clinic. After all, she was very pretty, and he liked attractive girls. He might have even been a little jealous when she later got married.

From the time he was about eight, Brad became very independent at his check-ups. Shane was a baby then and took a lot of my attention that Brad had been used to having. Brad started going by himself to the lab next-door to the clinic to have his blood drawn. Sometimes he would finish and wander back into the hall where the treatment rooms are to talk with friends and look for a room with a Nintendo game.

When video games first became widely popular, I told my kids not to ask for a set for Christmas because I felt they were a waste of time and money. Well, I entered a drawing at a local store and won first place: a Nintendo game set. So they got one anyway. After the hospital started having them available for the patients, I changed my mind about their value. Video games were the perfect diversion for Brad. He became so involved in playing that he hardly noticed anything else around him. It distracted him from pain and boredom.

Eventually the new Super Nintendo game sets were installed in a few of the treatment rooms at the clinic. Those rooms were supposed to be reserved for patients recovering from bone marrow transplants. By the time Brad was a teenager, transplants were being done locally on a large number of patients. If his diagnosis had come ten years later than it did, we may have chosen that treatment for him. Brad was almost always able to convince a nurse to let him use one of those rooms for his check-up and IV infusions, so that he could play the newer games. They began to save him a room on the days they knew he was coming for treatment. Occasionally Brad got himself set up in an examination room and was done with his check-up before I even knew that he had finished having blood drawn in the lab. I needed to remind him to come and find me before he saw a doctor so that I could hear the results of his exam and get answers to my questions.

Amy worked as the child life specialist at the clinic for about five years, then she and her new husband decided to move back to Alabama for his business opportunities. During her last year in Utah, I was pregnant with our seventh child. We really wanted another child to grow up with Shane. Some of the hospital staff thought I was trying to have a baby that would be a perfect match for a bone marrow transplant for Brad, but that was not the case. We just felt Shane would be happier with a sibling near his age, since he was seven years younger than Brad.

Twenty-one weeks into the pregnancy, I felt something was wrong. I insisted that my doctor see me, and Dave accompanied me as I went to have an ultrasound, which revealed what I had feared. The baby had died. It was a tough blow to our family. We had looked forward to having this baby girl, whose name was to be Karen. The next day, Dave and I went to the hospital where labor was induced. The baby was medically borderline between a stillborn and a miscarriage, so it was our choice whether to have a burial or leave her body at the hospital where she was delivered. After consulting with our bishop and stake president, Dave and I decided to have a burial. Our decision was influenced by Brad's situation. I didn't want him to think, if he did get sick enough to be facing death, that we would just leave his body at the hospital and forget about him.

We decided to call our baby Karen Amy, in honor of the Amy from the clinic who was such a good friend to Brad. Our family had a small graveside service for her. We spent many Sunday afternoons visiting the cemetery, bringing flowers, taking walks, and feeding the ducks in the adjoining pond. Brad learned that we do not forget members of our family, even when separated by death.

When Amy moved to Alabama, Stephanie (Steph) and Maren took over in Child Life. Steph was there during the majority of Brad's appointments. She went out of her way to learn about his friends and social life and had a real interest in him as a person. She came into the treatment room with Brad and me while he had spinal taps and bone marrow aspirations.

Because Brad was a cancer patient, our family was invited to participate in many activities throughout the years that were sponsored by the Candlelighters organization, Make-A-Wish, and the Cancer Wellness House. One event was the Ducky Derby, a major fund raising event for Make-A-Wish. For several years it was held at Lagoon Amusement Park. People in the community purchased rubber ducks, which were raced through the "lazy river." The owner of the winning duck won a car. Our kids volunteered to be "duck wranglers" and herd the ducks in the right direction through the water. A picnic and party for Wish Kids and their families was held in conjunction with the fundraiser.

Nathan's Eagle Scout service project was to provide a carnival for the kids at the Ducky Derby party. He made games and collected prizes and then had the other boys in his troop come and help run the carnival. Brad did the same thing for his Eagle project two years later. It was meaningful to our boys to give back a little to an organization that did so many kind things for our family.

The Candlelighters, a branch of the American Cancer Society that serves childhood cancer patients and their families, also provided parties and activities. Their annual Christmas parties were a highlight for our family. There was food, entertainment, and a visit from Santa, who took the time to talk to each child, pose for pictures, and give them a special wrapped gift.

The Cancer Wellness House is another place that provides help and support to those dealing with cancer. One year they held an Easter egg hunt, which we decided to attend. Brad was twelve years old, too old for the egg hunt, but not for refreshments and visiting friends. Shane was five, the perfect age to hunt Easter eggs. Once the party started, though, Brad decided maybe he wasn't too old to participate in the egg hunt after all. Sometimes it paid for him to be short and blend in with the eight-year-olds. He and Shane had a great time, snatching up their share of candy-filled plastic eggs. When the hunt was finished, there were muffins and juice for refreshments.

We were standing around the patio, eating and visiting, when Brad came over to me.

"Mom, I think there was something wrong with that milk I drank," he said quietly.

"Where did you find milk, Brad? I thought there was only juice."

"It was in that carton on the table," he said, pointing.

Janene and I both looked at the table and started to laugh.

"Brad," giggled Janene, "that's not milk. You just drank a glass of half and half. It's for people to put in their coffee."

Once he realized it wouldn't poison him, Brad was as amused by his mistake as the rest of us, and we laughed about it all the way home.

Chapter 16

ANYTHING BUT BORING

Brad was a very appreciative movie viewer. If producers hired professional audiences at premier nights to act impressed with their work, they would have gotten their money's worth out of Brad. I could tell from another room when Brad was watching cartoons, because he giggled through the entire program. He watched too much TV, too many videos, and played too many electronic games. But these were great distractions for him during treatments or at home on days when he didn't have the energy to play, or if his head hurt too much to even do homework. When it came to TV-related activities, he was completely absorbed in the show or game; he didn't notice anything else that was going on around him. He didn't hear conversations or respond to questions.

Maybe it was the depth of concentration he focused on the shows he watched that made it possible for him to remember the lines of movie dialogue. He struggled to remember how to spell words or do math, but he could quote entire segments of his favorite movies. He and Janene bantered dialogues back and forth, each quoting the next line from shows they liked. Some of Brad's favorites included *Top Gun*, *Independence Day*, *Space Jam,* and *Cool Runnings*. He liked the *Star Wars* series as well. *Forest Gump* was just made for quoting, and he often took advantage of that.

One line he picked up was from *Monty Python and the Holy Grail*, which he watched with Nathan and his friends. It must be a guy movie. I thought it was incredibly stupid, but they loved it. I believe he misquoted the line, but he loved to say, "I'm not quite dead yet," then giggle hysterically. To me, that quote became a symbol of Brad's life. He was definitely not quite dead. In spite of his health issues, he lived with enthusiasm, participating in life to the fullest extent that he was able. He didn't waste energy worrying about statistics or the probability of his life being short. He was just himself, a happy little guy enjoying life and reminding us often, "I'm not quite dead yet."

Brad's Journal Entry, July 2, 1996

Today I went to the best movie ever. This movie will make a man out of you. It was called "Independence Day." It's about aliens taking over the world. It was great. I can't wait to see the movie again.

LIST YOUR FAVORITE MOVIES, By Brad Coles
October 21, 1998

1. *Tommy Boy, because it is nothing but comedy*
2. *First Knight, because it is medieval type stuff*
3. *Cure, because it explains about things I have to go through*
4. *Hunch Back of Notre Dame, because I think this is the best Disney cartoon they ever made*
5. *Rocket Man, because it is so funny to watch*
6. *Mission Impossible, because it is a spy movie and it's tense*
7. *Space Jam, because of all the cartoon characters*
8. *U.S. Marshals, because I love the action in the movie*

9. *Fugitive, because it keeps you on your feet*
10. *Monty Python and the Holy Grail, it is one of those movies that you can laugh all the way through*
11. *Independence Day, because I like alien movies*
12. *Jurassic Park, I like dinosaurs and I liked how they put it together*
13. *George of the Jungle, because it is so realistic*
14. *Apollo 13, it is one of the best real life movies in the world*
15. *The Sand Lot, it is the best movie done about a bunch of kids*

Brad seldom complained about his illness. I often wondered if he was in pain. He had been sick for so much of his life, maybe he didn't remember what it felt like to be really well, healthy, and full of energy. On days when he felt lousy, if I asked him how he was doing, he said he felt "so-so." When he was really sick, he'd say, "I'm not feeling so good."

Just as he didn't spend a lot of time thinking about sickness or pain, he rarely talked of dying, even though he knew he might face an early death. During one period of time, though, he did have recurring fears about death. It was the summer he was nine, after his second relapse.

Brad understood our beliefs about death. He knew that our spirits are eternal, and death on this earth is only the death of our physical bodies. He knew that because of the Resurrection of Christ, all will be resurrected, body and spirit reunited. We taught him that spirits that leave this world go to the spirit world to be in a place of rest with Christ and loved ones that have died before.

Brad accepted these beliefs, but he began to wake up at night feeling worried about the unknown. I went to his room when he called and lay next him on his bed, trying to answer his questions and calm his anxiety. I assured him that when people died they are not alone, and if we live righteously, our family will be together, forever. When he went back to sleep, I returned to my bed, wondering if I had helped eliminate any of his concern.

One night he called me to his room.

"What's wrong Brad?" I asked.

"I'm having those thoughts again," he replied.

"You mean the ones about what happens when you die?"

"Yeah, I don't really get it."

"What questions do you have?"

"Well," he said, "I know that when your body dies your spirit is still alive. Then some time you get resurrected. Then don't you ever die again?"

"No, Brad, you don't. After you are resurrected, you live forever." I thought what a beautiful, reassuring principle that was.

"Well," Brad continued, his thoughts obviously taking another direction, "won't that be kind of boring?"

I must admit, I had never thought about getting bored with heaven, but he had a point. Forever does seem awfully long to those of us dealing with time. However, now that Brad and many of his friends are in heaven, I'm sure it is anything but boring there.

Brad got up one morning with a "shiner." His eyelid was purple and swollen, so he had to lean his head back to see out from under it. He couldn't remember being socked in the eye or even bumping into anything. It looked to me like a blood blister. I was tempted to try and drain it out, but decided not to risk anything without consulting the experts. Standard procedure when something unusual happened with Brad's health was to call the oncology clinic. "Bring him in," they said. "We'd better have a look."

We went to the hospital where Brad was a little embarrassed by the level of interest his eye was attracting. First Amy, his child life friend, looked him over.

Then the volunteer who weighed him in, the phlebotomist in the lab, several nurses, and finally a doctor all came to the same conclusion. Brad's eyelid was bruised-looking and swollen shut, and they had no idea why. Blood tests were normal; there was no fever to indicate an infection. Still, to be safe, the doctor decided he should be hospitalized until someone could come up with a reasonable explanation for Brad's sudden resemblance to a prizefighter.

It was summer, the hardest season to be trapped in the hospital. Brad and I went upstairs to be admitted for an undetermined length of time. He settled in with a video game, I with a book. That evening when Dave came after work for the hospital night shift, inspiration hit me---the girls could take turns staying with Brad! He wasn't sick, and they were lots better at video games than either Dave or I. It would be like a slumber party for them.

Our daughters were excited with the idea of being in charge of Brad overnight. Kristi volunteered to be first. That sounded like a good idea, since she was, as one of Nathan's friends had once pointed out, "a woman in control." The success of her shift would determine whether we would let the other girls stay. Kristi's night went smoothly, and Janene begged to be next. Now I was a little more hesitant. I had visions of her racing Brad through the halls in a wheelchair, or them trying to see how many positions a hospital bed could change into. She promised to behave herself, though, so we let her have a turn, and Brad loved having her there to play with him.

The third night was Alisa's turn to stay. Brad's eye still looked the same, and no diagnosis had been made for the cause of the problem. He had to remain at the hospital, receiving IV antibiotics, until somebody decided he could leave. Alisa took her Brad-watching duty very seriously. She was serious about most things, but determined to loosen up, play games, and entertain Brad for the evening. Dave and I were at home with the other children when the phone call came from Alisa.

"Mom, Brad's eye is bleeding!"

"Is it his eye or his eyelid?"

"I don't know---blood is gushing out of the corner of his eye!"

"Did you call the nurse?"

"Yes, she is in here now."

"Is she worried?"

"I don't know."

"Well, it sounds like the blister finally popped. As soon as it drains, it will stop bleeding. Is Brad doing all right? Let me talk to him."

Brad was less nervous than Alisa, but maybe things looked more gruesome from her vantage point. The bleeding was slowing down, and he was anxious to get back to his game. I spoke with the nurse, who came to the same conclusion I did about the blister popping. I told Alisa to relax and enjoy the rest of the evening and call me if Brad had any more problems. He didn't. The next morning his eyelid was deflated, but still purple. Since the cause of his hospitalization no longer existed, he was released to go home. It was many weeks before his eyelid color looked completely normal.

"HOBBIES AND INTERESTS," excerpt From Brad's Autobiography, 1992

I like to play soccer. My team wins most of the games. I collect trolls. I have twenty-one or twenty-two of them. I like riding my bike. I like to play Nintendo, but my mom doesn't let me play it too much.

I like to go on trips to fun places. I have been in twenty-two states, but I was too little to remember some of them. I save post cards from all the places I visit. My favorite trip was to Disney World in Orlando. That was my trip from Make-A-Wish. Swimming is one of my favorite things to do. I swim at my Grandma's and go snorkeling in Hawaii.

I like to go camping and fishing. I usually catch lots of fish with my grandpa. In the winter I have fun playing in the snow. I like earning awards in scouts. I am a Webelo.

Alisa graduated from high school in 1993, the same time Brad was finishing fifth grade. In the fall she left home to attend Ricks College in Idaho. For the first time, our family was getting smaller instead of larger. It was strange to have an empty bedroom. All the other kids volunteered to take it over, but we left it open for Alisa to come home on vacations and to use as a guest bedroom, something we had never had before.

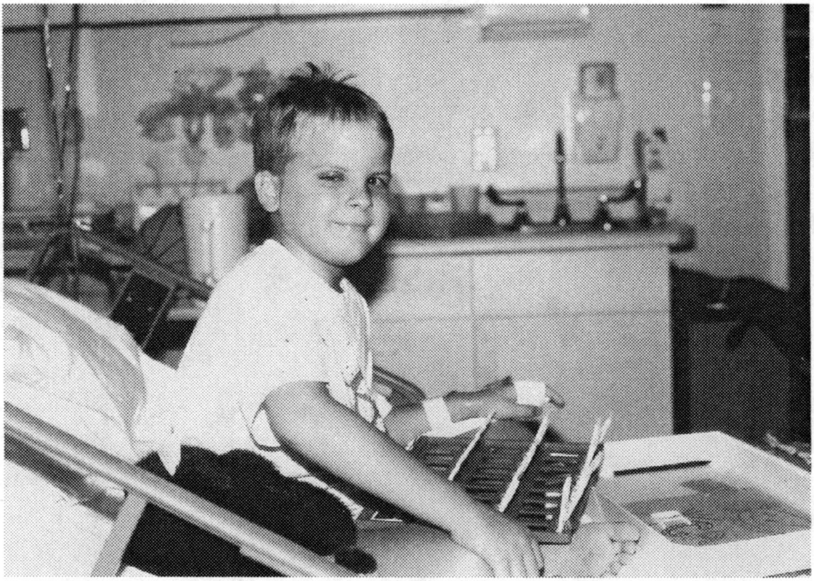

Bradley in the hospital with his swollen eye, 1992

Chapter 17

EVERYBODY IS NICE TO ME

On November 2, 1993, when Brad was in sixth grade, he had his next relapse. It was another central nervous system (CNS) relapse, meaning the leukemia cells were found in his spinal fluid, but not in his bone marrow. At this point, there was no standard treatment protocol for the doctors to follow as he had already been through those. The medical staff held a meeting to decide which drugs to give him and in what order. Their best guess was that if things were changed around somewhat, he might still respond to chemotherapy.

To treat the spinal fluid, the frequency of his spinal taps was increased. He was unable to take some of the drugs that had been included in previous protocols because he had developed allergies to them. With the remaining choices of chemotherapy drugs that are known to be effective against leukemia, the doctors came up with a custom-designed protocol for Brad. He was not required to stay in the hospital for reinduction this time because he was getting the same drugs he had been taking for years, just in different combinations and amounts.

He continued on the same treatment for the rest of his life, with doses being increased for a time whenever he had a relapse. It proved so effective for him that one of the doctors told me they had named it "The Brad Coles Protocol" and that they were testing it on other patients who had relapsed after finishing the standard treatments, hoping to prolong their lives as well.

We felt that perhaps the effectiveness of this treatment was due not just to the medication but also to the power of prayer. Brad had dozens of prayers being offered for him each day.

Shortly after this relapse, Bishop Oldroyd called for a fast by the members of our ward. Because it was a weekday, we did not expect a large number of people to participate, or even to be aware of the fast. We were overwhelmed that evening when we gathered in the chapel to end the fast: the whole room was full. We knelt together in prayer. The power of the Spirit was strong, as we felt once again that the Lord knew Brad and was in charge of his life.

Brad's seventh grade year meant a change to middle school, which is not usually the easiest transition in any child's life. At Quail Hollow Elementary School, nearly everyone knew Brad, knew about his health and his learning limitations. At Albion Middle School he would have to start over. There would be students from several other elementary schools and seven class periods a day, each with a different teacher. Each of those teachers would need to be informed about his illness, the resulting learning disabilities, and that he would miss school frequently for hospital visits. I talked with the principal, who felt I should meet with all of Brad's teachers and explain things to them as a group. We scheduled the meeting for the first week of school.

During the summer I became more and more anxious about Brad going to middle school. He would be the fifth child in the family to go, and all the others had survived, but not without some occasional problems. Alisa had been pushed around in the crowded hallways because she was small and not very assertive. Brad was also small, but maybe a little too assertive for his own good. Nathan, who was tall and strong for his age, had still been bullied in gym class for a short time. There were real reasons for concern.

For two class periods each day, Brad would attend a resource class to receive extra help and have the teacher monitor his progress. While resource classes at Quail Hollow had proven to be good for Brad, I wondered if he would have the same experience at Albion, or if he would be in a room full of gang members and drug users who would then become his best friends.

Brad had different things to worry about that summer as he prepared for middle school. He wanted to look good. He experimented with hairstyles, taking great care to comb it just the way he thought it should look. His hair had not fallen out completely with the addition of more drugs after the last relapse, but it was a lot thinner. The nurses at the hospital teased him about how handsome he looked and that his hair was going to break off because of the amount of styling gel and hair spray he used to make sure it stayed in place.

Finding the right clothes was also important to Brad. They didn't need to be expensive, but they did need to make a statement, and if they happened to be a popular name brand, so much the better. Finding pants to fit was a challenge. With his waistline constantly shrinking or expanding as a result of steroid treatment, pants that were the right size one day might not fit the next. His short legs added to the challenge. Little boy sizes fit better than adult sizes, but he had a young man's taste in clothes and didn't want to look like a little kid. It's a good thing he liked to shop, since we usually had to visit several stores to find something to make him happy without exceeding my budget.

One day near the start of school, I was talking to Brad again about my concern over the things he might have to face at middle school. "The kids might push you around because you're small," I told him. "You'll have a different teacher for every class. None of the kids from the other elementary schools know about your leukemia. You need to realize it won't be the same as elementary school."

He looked at me patiently, as if he were the adult and I the child and reassured me, “Mom, don’t worry about it. I’ll be fine. Everybody is nice to me.” Well, with that kind of attitude, who wouldn’t be nice to the kid? He was right. The faculty and the other students treated him kindly. He kept the good friends he had always had, adding new ones as well. There were some seriously troubled students in his resource classes, and he got along with them but kept his own values strong. He was treated just as he expected, which is true of most things in life. The way we look at ourselves goes a long way in influencing how others view us.

Brad usually walked to Albion, which was just a block farther up the street from Quail Hollow. Nathan was a ninth grader. Sometimes he and Brad walked together, but usually they preferred to go with their own friends. After school, if I timed it right, I could look out my bedroom window and see Brad coming home with his friends, all girls and all several inches taller than he. Trisha, Sarah, and Tara were his usual contingent of ladies on the walk home. They became his closest and most faithful friends all through middle school and high school. As the boys his age became involved more in athletic activities, there began to be a wider gap between what they and Brad were able to do. The girls were less competitive and liked him for himself. Besides, he was very cute and had a great sense of humor.

On weekends he got together with the girls to play games or watch videos. Our older kids were a little annoyed by this, since we had a strict family policy of no dating or boy-girl parties until they were sixteen. Brad was only twelve. Most rules have exceptions, and we made one for him, since he was with his best friends, not on a date, and he was generally the only boy with three or more girls.

At the time Brad started middle school, Kristi left home to attend Brigham Young University. This was our second child to leave home in two years, quite an adjustment for our family. It was especially difficult for Janene when Kristi moved out. They had shared a room for the past few years and were very close friends.

In high school, Kristi had dated Scott. He left to serve a two-year church mission soon after she went to BYU. Brad thought Scott was the greatest. Besides being quite short, a size that Brad could relate to, he treated Brad like a friend. After Christmas break, Kristi went back for her second semester at BYU and met someone new. Brad took this turn of events as a personal insult and remained a faithful friend to Scott, even later when Kristi and Curtis Johnson became engaged. It took many hours of Backgammon (which he let Brad win) and some wild wally-ball games for Curtis to convince Brad that maybe he was okay. Kristi and Curtis were married in August 1995.

Chapter 18

MOMENTS OF FAME

Brad got a lot of press coverage throughout the years he was on treatment. He loved the media attention. One year he was asked to appear in a commercial to promote Camp Hobe. It would be shown on local TV as part of a fund raising campaign for the camp. Janene and Nathan, as regular campers, were also invited to participate. The filming was done during school hours, which meant yet another day of missed class time, but it was for a good cause.

The commercial was filmed at Wheeler Farm, a nearby county park. Our kids, along with a dozen or so others, were supposed to pretend that they were at camp, having lots of fun. Never mind that Camp Hobe had no animals or hayrides, or that Wheeler Farm had no swimming pool or campfires. The kids had a great time. When the commercial aired some time later, Brad loved people coming up and saying, “Hey, Brad, I saw you on TV!” My aunt called to tell me that she had seen Brad on a commercial and was surprised to find out that I already knew about it. Maybe she thought that he had sneaked out of school without my knowledge and was living a secret life as a movie star. For months, whenever the commercial was shown, she would call me again to say that she had seen Brad on TV. It’s great to have a star in the family.

When Brad was in seventh grade he wrote an essay about his experiences with cancer to submit as a contest entry to the local chapter of the American Cancer Society. It was chosen as one of the winning entries, and as a result, Brad became a Junior Ambassador for the American Cancer Society for the coming year. The duties that honor entailed were somewhat vague. Basically, he and the other four Junior Ambassadors were to show up at fund raising events and look cute so that people would give more money. He loved it.

To start the year, the new ambassadors were invited to a private meeting with Utah Jazz basketball star, Karl Malone. Brad was a great fan of the Jazz and thought of himself as a pretty awesome basketball player. His favorite player on the Jazz was John Stockton, because in comparison to the other players he looked short. At the meeting, Karl Malone did a brief interview with the press and then dismissed them in no uncertain terms, so he could spend time with the kids. He talked with each one individually, gave them an autographed basketball, and posed for pictures. He asked Brad about his interests. Brad told him he was a fan of Forty-Niners football, especially Steve Young, and that he loved country music. Garth Brooks was his favorite performer. Karl told Brad he was a friend of Steve Young and Garth Brooks and that he would tell them about Brad.

A short time later we got some mail addressed to Brad. One envelope contained an autographed photo of Karl Malone, the official picture used for the Olympic basketball team that year. Another envelope contained a picture of Garth Brooks, on which he had written a message of encouragement. We framed both pictures and put them in Brad's room, next to his poster of a red Lamborghini. Though Steve Young did not send a picture Brad remained a loyal fan.

Throughout the year he was invited to various fund raising activities and promotional events. I accompanied him and the other ambassadors to the governor's office at the state capitol to deliver flowers as a kickoff for the "Daffodil Days" campaign. The governor was not in, and the secretary didn't know quite what to do with us but tried to make the kids feel welcome. We went to the "Run for Life Relay" where Brad participated in an honorary lap around the track with other cancer survivors and patients. Brad, Dave, and I were filmed for a spotlight on the Miracle Network telethon. That was definitely my least favorite activity. A friend of our family who is a TV news reporter did the interview. She tried to make us feel relaxed, and it worked great with Brad, who had never been nervous in the first place. But I kept wondering about which camera I was supposed to be looking at and worrying about saying something stupid on TV.

A major fund-raising event for the American Cancer Society that year was a gala dinner and silent auction held at a downtown hotel. I am definitely not part of the cocktail crowd and felt a little out of my element as we mingled with the other attendees, invariably dressed in black.

We surveyed the items available for bid in the silent auction. Most were expensive and not very practical from our point of view, but it was fun to look. Then Brad saw the item he just had to have. It was an autographed picture of Steve Young! No one had bid on it, and the opening bid was just five dollars. We let him sign up, explaining that if it got too expensive we wouldn't buy it. After that he kept going back every few minutes to see if there were more bids. When someone put down a ten-dollar bid he was disappointed, but we agreed to bid fifteen. The same person upped the bid to twenty, and we went back and forth in five-dollar increments until it reached fifty dollars. We finally told Brad that was the limit. The other person was obviously not going to give up, so we would let them have the picture. He was disappointed, having come so close to finally getting his dreamed-of autographed Steve Young photo.

We enjoyed the dinner and the planned program. As we were finishing our meal, one of the Cancer Society officials came to ask Brad a favor. She wanted him to say a few words to the audience and just tell a little of his experience with cancer. Oh dear. Suddenly I felt like I was on the sidelines at one of Brad's sporting events, holding my breath that the coach would not expect more of him than he was capable of, and praying that the audience would not boo him. She didn't realize that even though Brad was thirteen, his brain functioned somewhere in the range of a ten-year-old. Brad, however, had hardly a moment's hesitation before following her to the podium. He was a born entertainer.

He went to the microphone and the illustrious, well-dressed crowd gave him their complete attention. Brad gave from memory a brief summary of the paper he had written to become a Junior Ambassador for the American Cancer Society. He thanked everyone for supporting the benefit dinner and urged them, not very subtly, to donate lots of money. As he prepared to finish his remarks, he made a major faux pas. The only place he had done any previous public speaking was at church. The way you end a talk there is to say "In the name of Jesus Christ, Amen." You can guess what Brad did. He started his closing sentence, "I say this in the name of---I mean, thank you."

The crowd laughed and then gave him an enthusiastic standing ovation. The Master of Ceremonies thanked him for his remarks and said, "We all know where you were going with that. Some of us have done the same thing." Later we heard they had received a record number of donations that night.

Sunday afternoon, the day following the benefit dinner, I got a phone call. The caller introduced herself and asked if I was the mother of Brad Coles, the boy who had spoken the previous evening at the gala dinner. I replied in the affirmative, and she explained that she and her husband were the ones who had won the bidding in the silent auction for the Steve Young picture. They had wanted it for their children who were also Forty-Niners fans. It was during Brad's little speech that she realized his was the other name that had been on the bid sheet. As she told her children about Brad, they decided that they wanted him to have the picture. Later that day this family we had never before met came to our door and handed Brad the gift. I was very touched at their kindness, and Brad was thrilled to at last have a Steve Young picture.

Brad's Journal Entry, March 7, 1996

Today I met Karl Malone. I am the ambassador of the year because my story won the contest for being it. And now I have an autographed ball and a picture of Karl Malone in his USA 1996 Olympic suit. I also got a letter from him. He is going to send me an autographed picture of Garth Brooks and maybe Steve Young.

MY LIFE WITH CANCER
And the Pains and Struggles with it

Brad's Letter of Application to be an Ambassador for The American Cancer Society, 1996

I have had cancer since I was two years old and now I am thirteen years old and believe me it has not been easy having leukemia. I have had some pretty bad things happen to me. I had a seizure that put me it the hospital, an infected eye that put me in the hospital for a very long time and one time I broke out in hives because of a reaction to a medicine.

When you have cancer sometimes you lose your hair. That was usually a problem for me because kids would bug me about it, but my friends would stand up for me if people teased me.

But having cancer isn't all bad. Every summer I go to Camp Hobe, which is a summer camp for kids with cancer. There is also the Make-A-Wish Foundation that lets you wish for anything you want in the whole world. And I have gotten to meet every Utah Jazz player, even Thurl Bailey all because of cancer.

If you think everyone that has cancer dies from it you're wrong. I have had cancer for eleven years and I am fine. I may be a little slow at some stuff, but I don't really care at all as long as I get to be with a group of friends. I have a lot of friends at school that know what I am going through because they have gone to school with me ever since kindergarten and they know all about me. I am kind of slow in learning because I have had radiation on my brain which burned out some of my brain cells. It's sometimes hard to learn some things, but right now I am doing quite well in school. Math is my best subject and I love to draw, paint, and to play sports, especially soccer, and to go snow boarding. And I love roller coasters and just living on the edge. I like country music and line dancing. My favorite country singer is Garth Brooks. My favorite NFL team is the Forty-Niners because Steve Young and Jerry Rice are the best football players.

When you have cancer you can make lots of friends at the hospital or at camps. I have made lots of friends while having cancer. Most of them are older than me. There is one that I would like to point out. Her name is Wendy. She had cancer just like me. I met her at camp, and we became close friends and we loved doing things together, but she died this year when her cancer spread to her lungs. My good friends at school are Jonathan, Scott, Ivy, Carly, Trisha, Tara, and Sarah. They have been really good friends to me while having cancer.

When you have cancer sometimes you can get tired or lose your energy, but if you keep yourself in shape you should be okay. There is one thing that you have to know and that is if you have cancer there will be a few bad times, but don't let them get to you. I have been through a lot of bad times like having four relapses (that's when the cancer comes back) and I had a good friend die from cancer and other stuff. I know it is hard to go on, but you need to think of all the good things you did with your family and friends and go on with your life.

One of Brad's TV Appearances as an Ambassador, 1996
(Left to Right: Dave, Diane, Brad, Carole Mikita)
Photo KSL-TV

Chapter 19

A RIDE IN A FIRE TRUCK

The idea of Dave and me taking a day off during the week to have fun by ourselves was not just unusual; it was unheard of. But for some reason, in February of 1996, we decided to go skiing, just the two of us, while the kids were in school. Maybe it was the weather that persuaded us to go. It was a "blue powder" day---fresh snow, bright clear skies, and no wind.

After getting the kids off to school, we drove the short distance up the canyon to our favorite resort. Our plan was to ski for a half day, then return home about the time the kids were getting back from school. We made run after run down the uncrowded hills. Without children who needed our help, we had a chance to actually concentrate on our own skiing for the first time in our married life. It was a pleasant surprise to discover that for a couple of out-of-practice, middle-aged people, we did all right.

When we returned home that afternoon, the message light was blinking on our answering machine. There was a message from our neighbor, Kaye.

"Hi. Now, don't panic because I think everything is under control. Brad had a little problem at school today. He had a seizure in one of his classes. The school called me, then Sandy (our other neighbor on the emergency calling list), and she went to Brighton High School to pick up Janene and Nathan. They are with Brad now in the emergency room at Alta View Hospital."

It was Murphy's Law. Every single day of Brad's school career but this one I had been no farther away than the local mall. Brad had had only one seizure four-and-a-half years before. In fact, he had not taken medication to control seizures for over two years, since there did not seem to be a concern about another one occurring.

I called Kaye to let her know we were back and to see if the information in her message was still current. She explained again what had happened and asked if we had seen a message from her on the message board at the resort. We had to admit that it had never occurred to either Dave or me to look at the message board.

We picked Shane up from school, then went to the hospital to find Brad. He told us that one minute he was sitting on his chair in pottery class, and the next thing he knew he woke up on the floor. The paramedics came and transported him to the hospital. The highlight of the situation from his perspective was that he rode in a fire truck, not an ambulance.

After talking with the emergency room doctor, we signed the papers for his release. I then took him to Primary Children's Hospital for examination by his doctors. They decided not to admit him to the hospital, but prescribed seizure medication and scheduled a CAT scan and spinal tap for the next day.

Janene's Experiences of That Day, February 8, 1996

I was called out of seminary so that the school secretary could tell me that my little brother had just had a seizure at school and he was on his way to the hospital and that they couldn't find my mom or dad. What a fun experience that was. Sandy Weiss had to come and pick Nathan and me up from school and take us home to get a car so I could drive to Alta View Hospital. Mom and Dad were up at Alta skiing, so they didn't even know anything was wrong. When I got to the hospital the first thing that Brad asked for was food from Arby's. What a funny kid. He is sitting in the hospital recovering from a seizure and all he can think about is Arby's. So what could I do? I went to Arby's. I remember how excited he was when I walked in with that bag. He always knew how to look on the bright side of things.

Brad's Journal Entry, February 8, 1996

Today in my pottery class I had a seizure. It was not fun. I had to spend my day at the hospital, because my parents were skiing. Tomorrow I have to go back to the hospital again to get a cat scan and an L.P.

At Albion Middle School, teachers select students each term to be recognized as "Knight of the Quarter." (The school mascot is a knight.) Usually students are nominated on the basis of academic achievement or outstanding leadership. When Brad was nominated, I assumed it was because of his cheerfulness in the face of adversity.

At an awards assembly, all the nominees were introduced, then it was announced that Brad was the winner. He was thrilled, but not surprised at the honor. He just went through life expecting to win.

Brad's Journal Entry, April 3, 1996

Today I was Knight of the Quarter. I got a plaque, and they took my picture. I didn't have to go to one single class, because after the assembly I went to the hospital. For Scouts we went to the park and played laser tag with Brad Crawford's guns. It was fun.

During middle school, Brad decided he was a country music fan. The main reason for this musical preference was that Janene was in a country music phase, and he idolized her. She was always willing to take him to the gym to work out, or to let him wear one of her soccer shirts. He wanted to be just like her.

On days when Brad had doctor appointments, I picked him up at school after his early morning classes. The first thing he did when he got in the car was switch the radio from my "oldies" station to country music. On the half-hour drive to the hospital, I tried to let him listen to music of his choice. I actually like some country music, but only in limited doses. We seldom got all the way to our destination before I had reached my country music quota for the day. We usually compromised on a soft rock station, since he claimed to like any kind of music except oldies.

Chapter 20

A ROOM OF HIS OWN

Janene graduated in 1996. She was making plans to attend Ricks College in the fall. Alisa was married that summer to Steven Liddiard. They met at BYU, where Alisa had transferred after completing her associate degree at Ricks. We now had two married children and their spouses all attending school at BYU. But when Kristi discovered she was expecting a baby, our first grandchild, she decided to work full time and help pay for Curtis' school so that he could graduate earlier and support their family.

Brad's Journal Entry, June 19, 1996

Today Alisa got married to Steven. We had to baby-sit his little brother and our cousins. We had lunch at the Lion House. The meal was okay. Then we went to the reception. That was very long. We decorated their car quite nicely. After they left, we took all the presents home and we are going to bed, because we are pooped.

In July we took Janene and the boys on a trip to Ohio where Dave had business meetings. We were able to visit the Kirtland Temple then drive to Niagara Falls.

We spent the fourth of July at Sea World of Ohio, watching a fireworks show over a lake in the park. We had a great time, but Brad seemed to be more tired than usual.

When we returned home, his blood counts were too low for chemotherapy. His doctors decided to do a bone marrow aspiration and lumbar puncture to check for possible relapse. Fortunately, the tests revealed no problems. His blood counts gradually improved, and he continued on his regular protocol.

Brad's Journal Entry, August 5, 1996

Today at 5:30 in the morning, I had to get a bone marrow [aspiration]. I was put to sleep for it, because they had to do two of them. The reason I got it was to double check my bone marrow to make sure I didn't have a relapse again. All went well there. I slept most of the day. A bunch of neighbors came and left food for us. It was great. Later that night we went for a walk. My dad had to leave again on business in Ohio. Well, I had better get to sleep. My back is kind of hurting.

Brad was devastated when Janene moved out. She left most of her soccer shirts and country music CDs at home for him. She also gave him her "Bad Hair Day" baseball hat. It had been a present to her the previous Christmas, but he loved it from the start and had borrowed it almost constantly from the day she got it.

There was one major compensation when Janene left home. For the first time in his life Brad now had his very own bedroom. As a fourteen-year-old, it had been challenging to share a room with his seven-year-old brother. He arranged everything in his new room carefully and made sure Shane knew he was not welcome unless invited. Being able to close the door and have privacy to talk on the phone, listen to music, or just enjoy the solitude was a luxury he had long anticipated.

Brad and Ashley Smith having fun at a youth social, 1998

Chapter 21

BECOMING AN EAGLE SCOUT

Participating in Boy Scouts was a big part of Brad's social life from the time he was an eight-year-old Cub Scout until he achieved the rank of Eagle Scout at age thirteen. As a Cub Scout, he looked forward each summer to day camps at Camp Tracy in Mill Creek Canyon. There the boys worked on requirements for advancements and played in the dirt. They came home covered in dust or mud, depending on whether it was a dry or rainy summer. I went along as a chaperon sometimes and couldn't wait to get home and into the shower. I think getting dirty is a huge part of the appeal of Scouts for the boys. That, and lighting fires.

Brad loved to light fires. At Camp Tracy, he learned to stack sticks just right and where to place the match to start a roaring campfire. Once the fire was going, the objective was to keep adding stuff, the more creative the better. I heard stories of boys bringing Barbie Dolls stolen from their sisters to melt in the fires at Scout Camp. For dinners on camp outs, they brought something wrapped in foil to cook in the fire. Brad consumed many burned burritos and pizza pocket sandwiches over his years as a Scout. When he sat near a campfire, he always needed to have a stick in his hand, just in case something in the fire needed to be poked, which it invariably did.

The summer he was nine, after he relapsed for the second time, Brad was released from a stay in the hospital on the day when he was scheduled to be at

Camp Tracy with his Cub Scout Den. Our drive home from the hospital took us past the turn off for the camp, and he begged me to let him go join his friends for the rest of the day. I gave in. He was still very tired, but he spent a few hours in the cool woods of the canyon, forgetting that he was just coming home from several days of hospitalization. He didn't have the energy to stay the whole day, but it was a great lift to his spirits to be one of the guys again for an hour or two.

Some of the requirements for Scout merit badges are physically challenging, even for healthy boys. The requirements can be altered if necessary for those with physical limitations. Because Brad did not consider himself handicapped, it never occurred to him to ask for a modification of difficult tasks. He knew he wasn't as strong or as fast as other boys, but he felt he could do anything, if he just stuck to it long enough.

Dave made a point of being at all of Brad's Scout activities. He often planned early flights home from business trips in order to be back in time for a camp out. We didn't feel comfortable having a Scout Master be responsible for Brad during strenuous activities. His need for extra help, as well as the constant possibility of seizures, made it necessary for Dave to go with him. Fortunately, Dave loved going on Scout outings and spending time with our sons.

One merit badge that Brad's troop decided to work on together was the bicycling merit badge. Nathan had earned it earlier, so I knew how much work was involved. In addition to learning bike safety and repairs, the boys needed to complete five twenty-five mile rides and one fifty-mile ride. Brad was there for all the twenty-five milers, finishing all but one of them. He had gotten chemotherapy earlier the day of that bike ride, and just didn't have enough energy to complete the whole distance. During each ride, Dave stayed behind with Brad as the other boys raced ahead.

On one of the twenty-five mile rides, Brad was struggling even more than usual to keep up. He and Dave had been far behind the pack the whole way. They were so far back that they made a wrong turn at one point, but were able to get back on the right course by taking a parallel road. Dave asked Brad frequently if he wanted to quit, hoping he would say yes.

"No, Dad. I can do this," was the reply.

They peddled on determinedly, finally spotting the finishing point, a gravel parking lot where the rest of the group was waiting. As Brad turned into the lot, his tires slipped on the gravel, and he fell over, scraping up his hands and legs. The rest of the twelve and thirteen-year old boys responded in a way I would never have expected. Instead of laughing at him, or telling him how slow he was, they picked him up and carried him around on their shoulders in a dance of triumph. They were as thrilled with Brad's success as he was himself, and all of them shared in the victory.

The fifty-mile ride was scheduled for a Saturday. I felt it would be impossible for Brad to complete that distance, considering how he had struggled to go half as far on the previous rides. Before he left home, I encouraged him to do his best, but reminded him it was perfectly acceptable to quit any time he felt too tired. All morning I worried about how he was doing. When they finally returned home, Brad was exhausted but victorious. He had finished! Dave told me the story.

This ride was much like the others in that Brad and Dave rode at their own pace and were soon out-distanced by the other boys. It was important for Brad to go even slower than his normal speed to conserve energy. The space between them and the leaders grew greater as the time passed. Still, Brad was not going to quit. The farther they went, the slower he peddled, but the miles were gradually rolling past.

When they finally spotted the end of the route, Brad was once again given a hero's welcome. This time, the other Scouts lined up in two rows facing each other and created a tunnel for Brad as he rode the final yards to the finish. With cheering and "high fives," they all celebrated the completion of the merit badge requirements.

In order for the boys to receive the camping merit badge, a requirement for becoming an Eagle Scout, it is necessary to camp once a month, year round. Weather is not an excuse for canceling a camp out. In fact, for the boys it seemed to add to the fun to sleep out in a good snowstorm. I hated winter camp outs. Even though I was home in a nice warm house, I could not sleep all night, worrying about my sons freezing to death in a snow bank. Of course, Brad attended every winter camp out, and Dave went as well. There was one night it was so cold that they gave in to common sense and slept in the van, running the heater occasionally to thaw.

Backpacking trips presented a challenge for Brad. He was much smaller than the other boys his age, and the weight of a loaded pack was equal to about one third his body weight. And in spite of what he might have believed or told others, his muscles were weakened from years of medications. Brad's first backpack trip was to a lake high in the mountains, up a steep trail. Nathan went on that hike as one of his last scout camp outs. Carrying the pack was no problem for him, and as soon as everyone was out of the cars at the trailhead, Nathan and the other older boys took off to find the lake.

Dave and Brad took their usual place at the end of the line, accompanied by Brad Crawford, one of Brad's Scout leaders. They had gone no more than one hundred yards before it became obvious that Brad would not be able to make the hike while carrying his pack. Realizing that, Dave knew the only way Brad could go on this camp out was if someone else carried his pack. That someone was him. He took Brad's pack and wedged it onto his back, on top of his own, doubling the load. He never mentioned to Brad how heavy it was. They resumed hiking, Dave and Brad Crawford switching off periodically with the extra pack.

After spending a night in the beautiful mountain setting, cooking over a fire and fishing in the lake, they returned down the trail the next morning in the same fashion, Dave and Brad Crawford following Brad with his gear. Dave will be forever grateful for the help from Brad Crawford that made it possible for Brad to go on that hike.

Brad and Jonathan Roatcap at their Eagle Court of Honor, 1996

Chapter 22

QUEST FOR COOLNESS

One sport in which Brad could compete as well as anyone, at least anyone in our family, was golf. He wasn't very proficient at hitting long distances, but he was fairly accurate as far as direction. At least he was when we went to hit range balls. That is the only place I watched him golf, as I personally am not a golfer. Dave ruined my golf interest for life when, shortly after we were married, he took me with his entire family to play eighteen holes. I had never so much as held a golf club, unless you count miniature golf. I still have flashbacks of those few hours when all (and I mean all---at least a dozen) of my in-laws were alternately laughing at me or waiting impatiently for me to catch up.

So when our boys became interested in learning to golf, I decided this was a wonderful father-and-son bonding time. It actually worked out perfectly, since the girls and I could hit the garage sales on Saturday morning while the guys were trying to knock miniature balls into tiny holes at impossible distances.

Dave, though actually a pretty good golfer himself, does not keep score. If the balls go into the rough, he and the boys hunt around and find several extra balls, always coming home with more than they left with. How many golf balls do you actually need, anyway?

Grandma and Grandpa Taylor always brought their clubs when they came to visit during the summer and took Brad to play on our local par three course. After spending his first sixty years making fun of "goofers,"

Grandpa, in his retirement years, became one of them. Brad had his own set of clubs, inherited from his younger, but taller, girl cousin when she outgrew them. He didn't seem bothered at all by the fact that they were in a bright yellow golf bag. Brad loved to golf with his grandparents because they always rented a cart, which he was only too willing to drive.

At about age ten, Brad decided what he wanted to be when he grew up. He never questioned whether or not he would actually live to be an adult. He just started preparing for his career, which was to be a cartoon artist. He loved Disneyland, Disney World, and everything related to Disney, so he decided he would be a Disney cartoon artist. He practiced constantly, drawing cartoon doodles on his schoolbook covers, on notes to friends, on the printed program at church. He liked to draw goofy-looking faces, and could do a number of different ones quite well. Recognizing his limitations in some academic areas, Brad found something he could do as well as anyone and prepared to make that his future career.

Another area where Brad excelled, or at least competed fairly well, was in wood shop class. During seventh grade, all the students at Albion Middle School were required to take a core curriculum, which included a rotation in shop. He enjoyed it enough to register for a more advanced wood shop class the following year. When the class did a project to make lamps using empty soda cans as the base, Brad got an idea. He wanted to use a Spam can and make a lamp as a present for Nathan, who was known at Camp Hobe as Spam Man. We got a can of Spam Lite, which he turned into a "Spam Light." It was such a hit with the teacher that he entered it into the annual arts festival at the end of the school year where it won a prize. It is destined to become a family heirloom.

THINGS I DON'T WANT TO BE WHEN I GROW UP
By Brad Coles, September 14, 1998

1. *Garbage man who picks up people's messes*
2. *Business man who sits in an office all day*
3. *The man who sticks his head in alligator's mouths*
4. *The Unibomber*
5. *Wanted for murder*
6. *The man who lives in the jungle and studies gorillas*
7. *The school librarian*
8. *The school custodian*
9. *A worker at a fast food restaurant*
10. *A dentist who has to put his hand in people's mouths*

THINGS I WOULD WANT TO DO OR BE WHEN I GROW UP By Brad Coles, September 15, 1998

1. *Go sky diving for the first time*
2. *Work for Disney as an animator*
3. *Work for Warner Brothers as animator*
4. *Start my own business*
5. *Get married, but not at least until age 25*
6. *Have kids, three boys, two girls*
7. *Move out of my parents' house*
8. *Buy lots of outdoor sporting goods*
9. *Get a house in California*
10. *Be an actor in Hollywood*
11. *Be a famous inventor*
12. *Be a famous skier*
13. *Be a famous snowboarder*
14. *Be a teacher at a college*
15. *Die a happy man*

Snowboarding became the craze when Brad was in middle school. Many of his friends were learning to snowboard, and he wanted desperately to try. He did know how to ski, sort of. Since skiing was an expensive outing for our large family, we went only about twice a year. Brad never progressed much beyond the beginner runs because his muscles were not strong enough for the more difficult hills. When he fell, he usually needed help to get up again. Snowboarding, I had heard, is harder to learn than skiing. I tried to discourage Brad's interest, but he refused to be deterred.

None of our other kids had any interest in learning to snowboard. They were happy to stick with skiing. Brad continued to express his need to try the new sport. He found out through friends at school about a special beginning snowboard program at a nearby ski resort. It was a reasonable price, but I was not willing to let Brad go alone, and no one else in the family wanted to try. Brad persisted once again, and found a friend, Tyler, who wanted to sign up for the program with him.

Dave and I discussed the idea and decided to let Brad give it a try. I talked with Tyler's mom, who agreed to drive the boys to the resort in the morning of the lesson, and I would pick them up at the end of the day.

Brad left early, bundled in layers and filled with high hopes. All day I watched the clock, and the gathering storm clouds. It was snowing by the time I drove up the canyon to retrieve Brad and Tyler. At the resort, I slogged across the slushy parking lot to the agreed meeting spot. No Brad. The beginners' lift was nearby. Attracted by scores of snowboarders who appeared to have no idea what they were doing, I walked that direction, reasoning that Brad must be among them. None of them were going anywhere fast, and more were sitting than standing.

Trying to pick Brad out of the crowd, I observed the procedure for learning to snowboard, which went something like this: stand up, point the board downhill (into the fall line), slide about ten feet, fall down. Hmmm, maybe I could learn to do that. Brad spotted me before I saw him, his white and purple "Mighty Ducks" coat blending in with the snow.

"Hey, Mom!"

"How's it going, Brad? Are you frozen yet?"

"No, this is great! Come and watch me!"

I told Tyler and him they could take one more run while I watched. They rode back up the chair lift, and it's a good thing it was a very short one. They followed the above procedure, inching down the hill, as I stood grinning in the storm. Brad was snowboarding! He had realized a dream. It didn't matter that he was on the bunny slope, sitting more than standing. He was a snowboarder, one of the cool guys.

Brad's Journal Entry, January 29, 1995

Today I went snowboarding for the first time at Brighton. I went with Tyler Dashner. We had a blast. I saw everyone from school because we had the day off and the teachers didn't. I forgot that yesterday was the Super Bowl. Dallas and Pittsburgh were in it. The final score was 17 to 26, Dallas.

When Brad was fifteen years old he decided he wanted to learn to play the guitar---the electric guitar. We already owned two acoustic guitars, which Dave plays, but Brad wanted to make NOISE. He was envisioning enough amps and bass to make the house vibrate. Knowing it was his biggest wish that year, Dave and I gave in to his constant "hinting" and bought him an electric guitar for a Christmas gift.

We thought Dave would be able to teach him the basics of cords, fingering, and strumming, but that didn't work out so well. Brad wanted a real teacher, so I signed him up for a guitar class offered through the community school program. I was actually pretty excited because there was a beginning French class offered at the same time and location. I have always wanted to speak French, at least well enough to interpret the French words I encounter in books I read. I was hoping to finally make sense of that language that seems to have far more consonants in the written words than are necessary for the way they are pronounced.

Brad slung his guitar strap across his chest, I tucked my notebook under my arm, and we embarked eagerly on our first evening of instruction. I soon found myself in a room full of students who had all had at least some high school French, and a teacher who was a native French speaker. I wanted to learn, really I did. But I wasn't getting it. High school German had come easily for me; I was fluent in Spanish. But French did not compute in my brain, at least not as it was presented in that class. The teacher started talking, the students started replying, and I still didn't understand why I shouldn't pronounce half of every word.

Brad had a similar experience in guitar class. All the other guitar students knew how to play at least a little, some of them quite well. He learned two notes, which he practiced faithfully during the coming week. We attended three weeks of class, were out of town the fourth week, and went back determined to stick it out. By the end of the eight-week course, Brad was pretty good at his two notes and I could count to five in French. It wasn't a total failure for us, but not exactly the outcome we had anticipated.

Soon after those classes ended, I saw an ad for private guitar lessons and arranged for Brad to take them. He loved the teacher and slowly but surely started to progress beyond his two notes. The teacher was a refugee from the 70's, full of mellowness and oldies music. But she let Brad choose the songs he wanted to play. He strummed loudly, singing along to the tune in his off-key voice, and feeling extremely cool. During the last year of his life his guitar playing became a source of pride for him.

Brad with his guitar, 1997

Brad snowboarding at Brighton Ski Area, 1997

Chapter 23

RIVER RUNNING

Brad often convinced us to do things that pushed the limits of our comfort level. He always pushed himself, choosing to, as he put it, "live on the edge." In truth, he was not really as near the edge as he wanted to believe. But for him, participating in many normal activities was a triumph over his physical limitations.

When the opportunity came up for the teenagers of our ward to take a river trip on the Snake River for Youth Conference, there was no doubt Brad was going. The only question was which parent would accompany him. I was willing, but it made more sense for Dave to go, since he would be stronger to help paddle the canoe, and he and Brad could sleep in the same cabin at night. The only problem was, Dave had paranoia about river running, perhaps justifiably developed through his own Boy Scout experiences of canoeing the Colorado River.

Finally, with many misgivings, Dave consented to go. Janene and Nathan went also, leaving a day later with the older youth, because the group was too large to be allowed on the river at one time. Janene went under protest, since she had graduated from high school and was technically no longer one of the "youth." We wanted her to spend some time away from her boyfriend, who Dave and I felt was not the best company for her.

The first day for each group was spent floating calmly through Teton National Park, where everyone had to be quiet so as not to startle the wildlife. They saw a variety of the animals and birds for which the region is famous. On the second and third days of the trip, everyone paired up to paddle canoes down the next section of the river. Brad had agreed before he left home that his dad would be his canoe partner.

After an early breakfast, Brad was excited and anxious to begin the canoe phase of the trip. He watched impatiently as others got into canoes, paddling off into the current. The water was flowing swiftly just a little way from the bank as they prepared to launch. Dave had Bradley get into the canoe first and then jumped in himself, shoving off from the bank. Since Brad wasn't yet seated when Dave jumped in, Brad lost his balance and tipped over the canoe causing both of them to fall into the river.

The Snake River is hypothermia cold. Fighting against the current, Dave grabbed Bradley, and they held to the side of the now upright canoe. One of the guides, in his own canoe, saw what was happening and paddled over to assist. Brad did not have enough upper body strength to lift himself out of the water. The guide heaved Brad up by the straps of his lifejacket and deposited him back inside the canoe. Dave was able to wrestle his own body over the side of the canoe, which the guide was holding steady, but not without supreme effort. No harm was done, other than to increase Dave's level of nervousness another notch. He was determined to stay dry the rest of the trip. He positioned himself on his knees, with his legs wedged under a crossbar. By pushing outward with his weight, he could stabilize the canoe and maintain balance. Of course, he caused himself great physical discomfort staying in that position, but they did remain upright the rest of the trip.

Throughout the day, they floated and paddled for about eight hours, Brad doing the floating, Dave paddling furiously to keep to the calmest parts of the river. Brad participated in water fights with kids in other canoes, but Dave threatened anyone who tried to tip them over with bodily harm. At camp that night, some conceded defeat, choosing to ride in the vans the next day rather than endure another day of paddling. Not Brad.

He told his dad, "You don't have to go with me in the canoe tomorrow. I can ride with one of my friends. I'm not too tired for another day on the river." Dave, whose muscles were screaming for rest, tried to discourage him, but Brad was determined to complete the river-running portion of the trip whether Dave came or not. Dave went.

Janene, following a day behind with the other group of youth, was sharing a canoe with her friend Nick. She paddled hard to show off her athletic abilities. After a few hours, the group decided to stop for a rest on the side of the river. As she stood up to get out of the canoe, she passed out. Her eyes rolled back in her head, and as my friend Julie Lewis, a chaperone, later explained to me, she appeared dead. Lisa Crawford performed first aid for shock, then Bishop Westbrook gave her a priesthood blessing.

After the blessing she regained consciousness and began to improve. She was driven in the support van to an emergency room in Jackson Hole, where the doctor thought she was probably dehydrated. She rode in the support vehicle the rest of the time and got lots of attention, which she thoroughly enjoyed. After returning home from the trip, she became more involved with a good group of boys from the river trip and spent less time with her boyfriend. Maybe her little "spell" was more than a mishap. Perhaps it was an answer to our prayers.

I received a phone call from the traumatized chaperones about Janene's experience before Dave and Bradley got home from their river trip. It is a good thing Dave didn't know about the incident while he was still on the river. He was worried enough just being responsible for Brad. Upon her return home, Bishop Westbrook escorted Janene to our door. He pulled Dave aside and whispered, "Dave, don't tell your wife, but I believe that through the power of the Priesthood your daughter's life was saved there on the side of that river." It was another miracle in our lives.

Brad with some of his friends (Clockwise from Brad: Sarah Andersen, Tara Debenham, Trisha Broderick)

Chapter 24

MORE SEIZURES

After Brad's seizure at school in eighth grade the day Dave and I were skiing, he continued to have them at random times during the remainder of his life. If he forgot even one dose of seizure medication, he was sure to have one. That was the case in ninth grade when he had one during seminary class. Fortunately, I was home that time and able to pick him up so that the school did not have to call the paramedics. It was embarrassing enough for him that his class knew about the seizure without emergency vehicles showing up with lights and sirens, making the entire school aware.

Though he didn't have any more seizures at school, he had several more at home, sometimes after he had gone to bed. When he was already lying down, at least he didn't fall. During a family vacation to Washington, D.C., in October 1997, he had a seizure in our hotel room on the final morning of the trip. The best guess I could make for treatment was to give him an extra dose of seizure medication and hope that he would be all right for the flight home. That morning, we continued with our plans to visit Mt. Vernon, making frequent rest stops so that Brad would not become overly tired. Seizures always left him exhausted.

In January 1997, Brad was invited to a friend's birthday party, so I took him to buy some helium-filled balloons for the birthday girl. As we walked to the front of the store to check out, Brad carried the balloons.

Suddenly I noticed that he was walking in a circle, as if trying to spin himself around and get dizzy.

My initial thought was that he was being silly. I started to tell him not to goof around in the store, when in the same instant I realized that he was having a seizure. I dropped the items I was planning to purchase and tried to catch him before he fell. I was able to keep him from hitting his head with full force, and I sat next to him on the floor, talking quietly to him as the seizure continued. A store employee stared for a few seconds, then asked what was wrong. I told him it was a seizure, and should end soon. Some people stopped to watch, moving a distance away. Mothers took their children out of eyesight so they would not be traumatized by the spectacle. The seizure stopped after a minute or two and Brad gradually regained consciousness. Amazingly, he was still holding onto the balloons. The employee who had been watching rang up our purchases as I sat with Brad and then helped us out to the car.

At home, Brad took some medication and rested for a while. After a short nap, he was ready to go to the party. I wasn't sure if I should let him go. He had no history of multiple seizures, so it was not likely he would have another one. But the one he'd had left him tired and weak enough that he should have spent the evening resting. Finally, I decided to let him go for a while, but I wanted someone to keep and eye on him. Without telling Brad, I phoned his friend Trisha and asked if she would call me if Brad had any problems. Years later, she told me she was nervous that entire evening, worrying that Brad would have another seizure and she would have to be responsible.

Brad's Journal entry, September 12, 1996

Today at school we had the SAT tests. They took forever. After the testing was done we went to first period, where the most exciting thing happened. I had another seizure in seminary. It happened because I forgot to take my Dylantin.

Brad's Journal entry, January 25, 1997

Today I did the most embarrassing thing of my entire life. I had a seizure at the store. And now I have a big bump on my head from falling on the ground. Tonight I went to Tara's house for a party. It was a lot of fun. We rented the movie, "Son-in-Law." It was funny. Now I am going to bed because I am very worn out.

Chapter 25

LET'S FISH!

Brad was a fisherman. Our family often went fishing together, but it was a rare occasion for us to actually catch anything worth keeping. That's really okay with me. My idea of a perfect day of fishing is to take a folding chair, a good book and a bag of licorice, and find a shady spot to sit and enjoy nature.

Brad's idea of fishing was something different. He liked to catch trout, the bigger the better. Fortunately, there were two people who were willing to take him fishing that knew how to catch the big ones: his Grandpa Taylor and Roger Roatcap.

Grandpa knew how to fish. I, along with my three sisters, learned the fishing rules (and there were many) as we were growing up. We had to get up long before sunrise and be at the lake while it was still covered with a layer of damp fog. We had to sit in our spots with our poles held at the correct angle from the boat to avoid tangling lines. Grandpa (my dad) decided how many colors of line should be let out, according to the estimated depth of the water. No more than three fishing lines were allowed in the water at a time. As we trolled slowly across the slate-colored water, I stared hypnotically at the end of my rod, bobbing rhythmically, indicating that there was no fish attached to my hook. When one person got a bite, everyone else reeled in their line as quickly as possible to keep the lines from tangling. When the day started to heat up, the fishing was over.

On one fishing trip, Brad convinced Grandpa to help him complete a requirement for his motorboat merit badge for Boy Scouts. He needed to drive a motorboat, performing certain tricky maneuvers, such as going forward, backward, and docking the boat. It's a good thing that Brad was one of the people with whom Grandpa had patience. Brad took over the controls, going "full throttle," since fast was his favorite speed. Unfortunately, his reflexes were not as fast as his driving speed. When he found himself headed directly for the dock, he panicked and was not able to turn the boat. Grandpa grabbed the wheel and averted tragedy, though it was a close call. Dave and Nathan, who were in the boat as well, were impressed that Grandpa kept the swearing to a minimum. They all agreed that Brad had done enough boat driving to pass his merit badge requirements.

Roger Roatcap, Jonathan's dad, was Brad's other fishing idol. The first time he offered to take Brad on an all-day fishing trip, I wasn't so sure it was a good idea, considering Brad's health concerns. Roger had shown Brad some of the monster trout from previous expeditions, and Brad begged to go, sure this was his chance for a trophy fish. Realizing how important this opportunity was to Brad, Dave and I consented to the trip.

Roger knew the rule about getting to the lake early and picked Brad up before dawn. They were gone all day and into the evening. When it had been dark one hour, then two hours, I began to get really nervous. Okay, I had been nervous all day, but now I was ready to call out the National Guard. It was after 11:00 p.m. when Brad finally came home. He was toting a load of huge rainbow trout, stuffed with junk food, and high on success. He could hardly wait for the next trip. This was, he was sure, how real men fished.

Years later, Roger explained why they had been so late returning from fishing that day. Their group had rented two fishing boats. Throughout the day, they followed each other around the lake, trolling into all their favorite nooks and crannies. When they finally began to make their way back to the dock late in the evening, the first boat ran out of gas. Roger threw a rope to his friends in that boat and was towing them to shore when his own boat ran out of gas as well. They were barely in sight of the marina, and no other boats were around. The sun had disappeared over the mountains, and it was growing cold.

Roger said that he looked at Brad, shivering in a blanket and silhouetted against the rising full moon. He asked him, "Brad, what do you think we should do?"

Without hesitation Brad replied, "Let's fish!"

That simple reply sums up Brad's attitude about many things in his life. There were things he could not change, but that did not keep him from taking advantage of the opportunities and good things around him. They did fish. Eventually the marina personnel realized they were missing two boats and went searching for them, rescuing the stranded fishermen and their bounty of trout.

When he turned nineteen, Jonathan Roatcap was called to serve a church mission in New York State and wrote our family a letter from his mission describing some of his experiences with Brad.

Excerpt from Jonathan's Letter, 2001

I know that Brad is with me everywhere I go. I can feel him walking down these long country roads with me, and he is touching these people before I even get to their doors. I know this is where the Lord wants me to be and I also know that this is where Brad would want to be. He always told me that one of his main goals was to go on a mission, and now I am sure he is accomplishing that goal.

I wanted to write you about some of the things that I got to do with Brad and some of my memories about him. Number one was his personality. He had a smile that would brighten anyone's day, no matter how sad you were. I know everyone says his laugh was infectious, and they were right. He had a way of changing the atmosphere in any situation.

I remember riding our bikes down to 7-11 and buying candy that we had to hide in our drawers at home because neither of us was supposed to go that far. We always thought we were so sneaky. Brad had a crush on Ashley Smith, and when we would jump on the trampoline and she came outside, he would be embarrassed and hide. The go-cart was a fun thing. He would always tear around going crazy, and I'm a fat guy, so it would tip. I still have scars on my arms from trying to push the moving ground to keep us from going over. Miraculously, we never did.

We would always go swimming at Alta Canyon. Those were always fun, churro filled days. He loved playing wally ball. He loved to play pool and could hustle anyone. He was the same at foosball and ping pong, and air hockey. He loved basketball, and I remember him always doing the very best he could at everything. He was never down.

My fondest memories were when we would go fishing. We had the most fun joking around, eating junk food, and catching hoards of fish. I could never figure out why he always, and I mean always, caught the biggest fish. I remember one time he almost went in with the fish pole and all. He was not going to let go. I had to grab his life jacket and anchor him in the boat while he and my dad reeled in a huge rainbow.

There are butterflies all over up here in New York.

Your friend, with love, Elder Jonathan Roatcap
P.S. I wonder if there are fish in heaven?

Brad catching a minnow on a fishing trip to Jordanelle Reservoir, 1997

Shane and Brad taking a ride on the go-cart, 1994

Chapter 26

NEED FOR SPEED

Dave put the idea of a go-cart into the kids' heads. When our old power lawn mower died, he saved the engine, telling our young children that he would help them build a go-cart and power it with the lawn mower engine, which he would repair.

Years passed. The dead lawn mower moved with us from California to Utah and took up residence under the worktable in the garage, where it remains to this day. It did not become a go-cart, but Dave and the kids continued to think about having one.

Dave seldom shops, unless he needs computer stuff or home repair items. So when he offered to take Janene, Nathan, and Bradley Christmas shopping, I should have been suspicious right away. I am sure that he had ulterior motives from the start. They returned home, without any shopping done, but with the thrilling news that they had found a go-cart for sale. Oh boy.

"Just come and look at it," they pleaded. "See what you think before you decide if we can get it."

The go-cart (they had a total of one in stock) was at a local sporting goods store. It was a two-seater model, built low to the ground, which the kids assured me would make it very safe. It was also very expensive. They insisted it was what they wanted for Christmas, even if they had to come up with part of the purchase money from their own savings, which they did, to prove to me that they were going to be responsible vehicle owners.

"We'll drive slowly," they said. "We'll take turns, wear helmets, and be careful."

On Christmas Eve the shiny black beauty made its debut. As our kids roared around the circle (not going slowly), the neighbor kids started showing up, one by one, drawn by the irresistible magnet of a power engine. Maybe money can't buy friends, but exciting toys sure create instant popularity.

Brad loved the go-cart. He was more prone than the other kids to drive too fast, not to slow for corners, and to forget about watching for cars. There was really nowhere that it could be driven legally. It was not licensed for the street and certainly not safe on the sidewalks. Occasionally I let the kids take it up the street to the parking lots at the church or the schools. Brad was not allowed to go there alone because I did not trust him. He was confined to driving around and around in our circle, giving the neighbor kids rides until most of their parents (wisely) banned them from riding with him.

As much as Brad enjoyed the go-cart, it was small potatoes compared with a real power machine, like a four-wheeler or a snowmobile. He had occasional opportunities to go riding with friends who owned them and always wished we could have our own.

We had the chance to take a snowmobile vacation to Yellowstone National Park the year Janene started college in Rexburg, Idaho, only a short drive from West Yellowstone. Dave and I and our three boys picked up Janene on our way.

We spent the night in a nice motel and enjoyed the hot tub. The next morning we were up early to get the most out of our snowmobile rental fees. I was relieved, and Brad, then fourteen years old, was crushed, that only licensed drivers could operate the snowmobiles in the park and a speed limit was strictly enforced. Janene and Nathan were legal drivers, so Brad volunteered to ride with Janene, sure that would be the next best way besides controlling his own machine to have some excitement.

We drove the route from West Yellowstone to Old Faithful, steering around bison in the road, as steam from surrounding geyser basins rose into the gray sky. We ate our picnic lunches in a heated building while we waited for Old Faithful to put on its show. It finally erupted, somewhat behind schedule, spewing plumes of steam into the atmosphere, ascending up against the falling snowflakes. The trip back to West Yellowstone seemed to take less time than it had on the way there. We left the park with several hours of time left on our rented machines. It was not difficult to find somewhere else to ride. Endless trails run throughout the area around West Yellowstone. We drove on some for a while with Brad begging, "Please, can I drive now? Please, please, please?"

We were riding in an open area of hills and gullies, and few real obstacles, so I decided it looked like a pretty safe place to give him a driving turn. I switched him places, hanging on in back as he revved the throttle. I'm not sure why I got to ride with him instead of Dave, or Nathan, or Janene. He went his favorite speed---too fast.

"Slow down!" I screamed over the roar of the engine. "I told you not to go fast!"

"I'm not going that fast," he insisted.

"Yes, you are. Slow down right now or your turn is over."

He did manage to find a more comfortable cruising speed, at the threat of losing his privileges. We played around until our time limit was used up on the snowmobile rentals and our thumbs were aching from holding down the throttle.

The trip was so much fun that the following year we went back again. This time the weather was clear and the sky a bright blue as we toured the park, then returned to town to finish up our riding time. Near the end of the day, Dave and I sat on a snowmobile at the side of a snow-packed field, watching Janene and the boys zoom around on the other two machines. They went out of view over a hill, and suddenly the machines got very quiet. Something must have gone wrong. Dave and I went to investigate and found our kids, laughing hysterically, picking up bits of colorful fabric from a trail in the snow. There was something familiar about that fabric.

I had brought along a duffel bag full of spare mittens, hats, and sunglasses in case someone got wet or lost something. The bag had been fastened with bungee cords to the back of Janene's snowmobile. Somehow it had slipped loose, gone underneath the machine, and been sucked into the engine, where the bag and its contents were turned to the confetti that now littered the snow.

Dave and I were not amused. It was not in our budget to buy a new snowmobile engine. Dave lifted the engine cover and inspected for damage, pulling out bits of black gloves, red duffel bag, and assorted other pieces the kids tried to identify. They couldn't stop laughing, even though I was mourning the loss of perfectly good snow clothing, and Dave was sweating the likelihood of engine damage.

When all the visible scraps were picked clean, Dave closed the cover and, as we all held our breath, started the engine. It worked! He took it for a quick spin to make sure it was all right, and then we lined up and headed for the rental facility. No more freedom for those kids. The first two machines checked out fine, as we knew they would. Then the attendant inspected the third one. He lifted the cover, looked inside, and closed it again, as all six of us breathed a collective sigh of relief. Funny how we all saw some bits of bright red fabric that the attendant had missed.

Brad's Journal entry, March 8, 1997

Yesterday I went to Yellowstone with my family. We picked up Janene on the way there. We stayed at the Holiday Inn. There was a hot tub and an indoor pool. Today we went snow mobiling. It was a lot of fun. We drove through Yellowstone and went all the way to Old Faithful. We watched it go off, then got back on the snowmobiles and left. We rented three snowmobiles. One was for Dad and Shane, one for Janene and Nathan, and one for Mom and me. I sometimes went with Janene, though. I got to drive one time too. Then we took the snowmobiles back and left to go home. We dropped Janene off at college. And now I am going to bed.

Brad resting on his snowmobile in Yellowstone National Park, 1997

Chapter 27

LOSING COUNT OF RELAPSES

On January 24, 1997, Kristi gave birth to her first baby, Emily. Dave and I became grandparents and Brad became an uncle. Kristi and Curtis were still living in Provo where Curtis was finishing his civil engineering degree. Brad wanted to go see Emily at every possible opportunity. He loved holding her and helping take care of her, and as she got bigger, playing with her.

Six months later, Alisa's first baby, Katie, was born. They also lived in Provo, so now there were two babies to play with when we got together for family activities. Brad loved being an uncle.

In February 1997, Bradley had yet another relapse. Only a few days earlier, he had learned of the death of another of his camp friends, making him highly aware of cancer's possible outcome. By this time I had lost track of the exact number of relapses, but it was around seven. Some years before that I had asked another parent how many relapses her child had experienced, and she said she wasn't really sure. Her answer shocked me. How could she possibly not know? I couldn't imagine losing track of such an important statistic concerning my own child. But now I was in that same situation myself. Since he continued to have CNS relapses, it was not always clear weather the blast cells found in his spinal fluid indicated a new relapse or if the cells were left from the previous relapse, and had not yet responded to chemotherapy.

Brad was no longer being started on reinduction phases of chemotherapy when he relapsed. Instead, he was given more frequent spinal taps with chemotherapy medications for a few weeks until the fluid was clean once again and then preceded with normal protocol. His hair thinned out with the increase in medications, but he never lost it again completely. I asked the nurse practitioner one day why his hair was thinning again, since his treatment at that time had remained the same for several months.

"You shouldn't be wondering why it is coming out," she said. "You should be wondering why he has any at all." He was receiving enough drugs on an ongoing basis to cause him to loose all his hair.

The years of chemotherapy were having a cumulative effect on many of the vital organs in Brad's body. His kidneys, heart, and lungs all showed signs of damage. He was issued an inhaler to help him breath more easily when he felt short of breath. His reflexes were slow. He broke out in rashes on his face, red bumps around his nose and on his chin. I wondered, if the leukemia stayed under control, how long his body could tolerate the poisonous drugs he had been receiving almost nonstop since age two.

Brad's Journal Entry, February 16, 1997

Today at church they divided our wards, and now we are in 8th Ward. It is brand new. Kristi, Curtis and Emily, Alisa and Steven came for dinner. Dad left for Kansas City again. I found out that Sharifa's little sister, Summer, died two days ago. There goes another one of my dear good friends that lost the fight with cancer. It STINKS! I saw Shane and Dixie Lewis tonight.

Brad's Journal Entry, April 28, 1997

Today I did a commercial for the National Cancer Survivors' week. It was a lot of fun. I watched the biology class dissect a shark for my journalism class. I called Emily today. Then Kara called me. I love having lots of girlfriends. It makes it so easy to pick and choose.

Brad's Journal Entry, June 4, 1997

Today was my last official day at Albion Middle School. It has been a great school year. Next year I will be in 10th grade and will go to school at Brighton High School. I got to go to Lagoon for my 9th grade trip. I spent the day with Tara, Trisha, Sara, Raylin Sarah, Adam, Tim, and Brett. We went on a lot of fun rides, even the Rattlesnake Rapids. I said good-bye to all my friends that are going to a different school or moving away. I came home about 12:00, so I am going to bed. It was the greatest year of my life.

Chapter 28

A TRUE PIONEER EXPERIENCE

The year 1997 was the sesquicentennial celebration of the arrival of the first Mormon pioneers in the Salt Lake Valley. Many people were reenacting wagon trains and handcart companies in honor of the original pioneers. Our stake youth leaders decided to organize a three-day handcart trek for Youth Conference that summer. The 350 or so teenagers, fourteen to eighteen years old, were divided into "families." Each family consisted of about ten teens and a married adult couple to serve as parents during the trek.

It was no surprise that Dave and I were asked to be handcart parents, since the only way Brad could go was if we went with him. It sounded like a fun adventure. Many of our ancestors had been pioneers, so we probably had a natural talent for such things. In preparation for the trek, we made or bought pioneer-looking attire. For the guys it was not so bad---jeans, a long sleeve, button-up shirt, and a cowboy hat. For the girls and "moms" it was another story. We had to wear full-length skirts with bloomers underneath, long sleeve blouses, and a bonnet or sun hat. We would be in the same outfit the entire three days since our limit of luggage did not allow for a change of clothes.

There were cooking clinics for the pioneer parents, so we could learn to prepare meals for our families in a Dutch oven over an open fire. Dave and I had to buy Dutch ovens, since we had never used them before. We stitched clothes and purchased water containers and numerous blue plastic tarps (standard pioneer issue, of course). All the participants attended meetings to learn some of the history associated with our stretch of the actual Mormon pioneer trail.

We arrived early in the morning at the starting point in western Wyoming. In a sagebrush-covered field the handcarts were lined up and waiting. The youth were assigned to "family" groups where they were with others they did not know well. A variety of ages and physical abilities were included in each family. Brad was the exception. He knew he was going to be staying in the group with Dave and me, but he would have preferred being more independent. Nathan was assigned to another set of parents. We rarely saw him the whole three days.

We met our family of eight new children and then loaded our handcart. It held surprisingly little, and our belongings were heaped up high above the sides, covered with the blue tarps, and then roped into place. We had three sons in addition to Bradley, and one of them looked kind of scrawny to me. That left us with two strong ones. There were five girls, one of them as strong as the boys. I felt guilty evaluating them on their physical attributes, like I was a slave buyer. Still, we had to move that handcart, and the strong ones were going to be important. Ropes attached to the front and back of the handcart gave everyone a place to push or pull.

The experience was not 100 percent authentic. We had portable toilets trucked in for our overnight stops. That may not sound like much of a luxury, but under the circumstances they were greatly appreciated. Of course, once again the guys had the obvious advantage in that department. Our food was delivered for each meal, so we did not have to hunt or forage, just start a fire and cook it in our trusty Dutch ovens.

For the first few hours, our handcart bounced along with relative ease. Everyone was fresh and energetic. Each group was ready to prove its toughness by out-pulling the others. The weather was pleasant, overcast and not too hot.

The first big challenge was a long, steep hill we had to descend. Handcarts don't have brakes, so we used the ropes to hold ours back and keep it from flying to a tragic death at the bottom of the hill. As it got close to lunchtime, the clouds thickened, and it began to rain. At the same time, we came to a wide, icy cold stream we needed to cross. No bridge. I was beginning to doubt my pioneer genes. We took off our shoes and socks, rolled up pant legs or held up skirts, and waded across. The handcart had to get across too, but my focus was getting Bradley to the other side. We were already getting a pretty good soaking from the rain; I didn't want him to fall into the cold water. The streambed was covered in slimy rocks that made footing tricky. I held onto Brad's arm, and taking baby steps, we inched our way across.

On the opposite bank, I wanted to get our coats off the handcart, since we were getting cold. I found that the tarps had not covered them, and they were soaked. Brad was shivering, and there was no place to get dry or warm. I admired those real pioneers more now. I was wondering at the wisdom of bringing Brad on this trip, but the storm passed quickly, and everything was soon dry. Then it got too hot. Fortunately we had the blessings of modern sunscreen and plenty of water. At every rest stop, we reminded the kids to drink and put on more sunscreen.

Accompanying all the handcart pullers were half a dozen leaders on horseback. The reason for them was to provide assistance to kids that might be having trouble keeping up. When one of the horsemen asked Brad if he wanted to ride for a while, of course he said yes. He was actually doing just fine walking, but riding sounded like a more exciting adventure. It was.

Since the horses were following behind the last handcart, we left Brad with them and kept walking. We walked several more hours through the rest of the afternoon, uphill and down, over sagebrush and rocks. On the way we passed markers indicating the graves of some original pioneers. Finally we arrived at the designated camping spot on the ridge of a barren hill. Tired and hungry, we unpacked cooking supplies and started our campfire.

About that time, some of the leaders from the final handcart, the medics for the group, came to find Dave and me. Brad, they explained nervously, had been thrown off a bucking horse, and his arm was injured, probably broken. Something had spooked his horse, causing it to buck wildly. Brad had held on as long as he could, they told us, then slid off and instinctively rolled out of the way of the animal's hooves.

As they described it, after the fall his face was ashen and his arm was bent in an awkward angle from his body. It began to swell and discolor, apparently broken. Gary Peterson and President Kennington were nearby and gave him a priesthood blessing. The nurse wrapped his arm in an elastic bandage, and they radioed the driver of the supply truck to pick him up. The truck was expected to arrive soon with Brad and our dinner supplies. They said that Dave and I should plan on taking Brad into Evanston that night for x-rays. That was an unpleasant thought considering I was dead tired, had hungry teenagers to feed and chaperone, and faced two more days of handcart pulling. Besides, we would look strange in an emergency room dressed like pioneers.

Brad soon arrived in the truck, which also carried the supplies for our dinner. We asked Brad how his arm felt, and if he had any other injuries. He thought everyone was making too big a deal of things and was a little embarrassed that he had been bucked off the horse. He assured us that his arm was fine, except that the elastic bandage was uncomfortable. The nurse was with us when Brad arrived and advised us to leave his arm alone until a doctor could examine him. Brad insisted it was all right, except the bandage was too tight. I carefully unwrapped the bandage to have a look. Amazingly, his arm appeared completely normal. There was no swelling, no bruising, no discoloration, and no pain.

Several of the people who had seen the fall and his purple, swollen arm, came to check on Brad's condition. They couldn't believe that his arm now looked fine. Dave later spoke with Gary, who had given Brad the priesthood blessing. He said, "The heavens opened to give me a knowledge of how special Brad was and that Heavenly Father was watching over him." Did angels cushion his fall so he wasn't hurt worse? Did the Lord answer prayer and heal his arm? Those who had seen his arm after the accident were sure it was broken, but it never bothered him at all after the blessing. However, he did choose to walk rather than ride a horse during the remainder of the trek.

The third morning of the trek I woke up with dirty clothes, dirty hair, and aching muscles. The stake president walked from camp to camp calling, "Bring out your dead! Bring out your dead!" Apparently he, like Brad, was a fan of Monty Python. I decided that if I had been a real pioneer I would have been tempted to turn around at that moment and go back. Instead, I got up and started breakfast. As I was cooking pancakes, a ball of flame shot up from the lid of the Dutch oven, which I was using as a griddle, singeing my eyebrows and hair. I was definitely not pioneer material. Later that day, finally back home and preparing to enjoy a hot shower, I found a tick embedded in my thigh. Dave had already found one on his stomach. He became sick for several weeks with what a doctor finally decided was Rocky Mountain Fever. That was the same disease Brigham Young had that kept him confined to a wagon at his arrival in the Salt Lake Valley. Dave had had the True Pioneer Experience. Brad and Nathan returned home tick free, and Brad's arm was fine.

Brad's Journal Entry, June 18, 1997

This last week I have been on a Pioneer Trek. It was a lot of fun. The first day I got bucked off a horse. It rained really hard. The next day it was really hot and almost everyone got a sunburn. Then today it rained in the morning and was sunny the rest of the day. I had a cool pioneer family. Our last name was Red-N-Bocker. We had a hoe-down last night. That was a lot of fun. Tonight it began to rain again. It was coming down hard and there was a lot of lightning and thunder. The lights went out at one time but came right back on. So I would have to say that the pioneer trek is a lot harder than I thought it would be.

Brad on the back of one of the horses during trek, 1997

Brad taking a rest during the Pioneer Trek, 1997

Chapter 29

THE BIG "16"

Becoming a Brighton High Bengal was another big milestone in Brad's life. He was excited, but a little nervous about going. His sisters and Nathan teased him about finding the "green door at the end of the hall." It was a joke used to give directions to unsuspecting new sophomores. Brighton was built in the experimental phase of school design, and its halls are circular: there is no end to the hall, and no green door anywhere. I could not believe he was ready to go to high school. For one thing, he was much too short, a source of unending frustration for him.

Brad became a faithful Bengal from the start, attending all the social activities and football games. His life-long friends, Sarah, Trisha, and Tara, were there, along with Jonathan and many others that had been important in his life for years. Brad was younger by several months than most of them, and as they turned sixteen and began to drive and date, he looked forward anxiously to his turn.

Brad's Journal Entry, August 25, 1997

Today was the first day of school for me at Brighton High School. Everything went pretty well for the first day. I didn't get lost once. I don't have very easy classes except seminary. There really aren't any cute girls in any of my classes, so it is kind of disappointing. Well, I have to go to bed now because it is very late.

Teaching our children to drive has been one of my worst traumas. Getting into the passenger seat and handing the keys to a fifteen-year-old is an act of great courage. With each of the kids, I put it off as long as possible, waiting until they were actually scheduled for driver's ed at school. Many people seem to not be able to wait until their kids drive. They hold them on their laps as toddlers and let them steer. By the time they are ten, they are backing out of the driveway. When they are old enough to get a license, they have more hours behind the wheel than their parents.

Our children, by contrast, go into driver's ed barely knowing where to put the key. When it could no longer be postponed, we took our oldest vehicle to the parking lot at the middle school up the street to give them diving lessons. On weekends the lot is empty, so there were few obstacles other than curbs and light posts, which at least hold still. Our old car had a standard transmission, which added to the excitement of the experience. A typical first lesson went something like this.

Me: "Put your right foot on the gas, the left on the clutch. No, not the brake, the clutch! Now, as you press down on the gas, slowly let up the clutch."

Child, after we lurch forward and the engine dies: "This car is a piece of junk. I did it just like I was supposed to, but it doesn't work right."

As we worked with Alisa, our first child, on driving skills I wondered, not for the first time, what ever possessed me to want six children. We had so much to look forward to. In fairness, I will admit that the kids all preferred their dad as a driving instructor. It bothered them just a little when I kept gasping in fright and covering my face with my hands. Somehow the oldest four managed to learn to drive. Then it was Brad's turn.

Because he had seizures, we knew there might be legal restrictions that would limit his driving privileges. To a teenager, there is no greater symbol of freedom and maturity than a driver's license with his picture on it. Brad wanted to drive. I tried to imagine him at the controls of our twelve-passenger van, straining to see over the steering wheel and reach the pedals at the same time. He was only four-feet-ten inches tall.

Brad went ahead with his driver's ed class at school. I had called the Department of Motor Vehicles, trying to find out the driving laws concerning a person who has seizures. It was only after he had completed his course that I found out he should not have been allowed to drive at all. There is a waiting period after a seizure in which a person cannot drive. If he could make it six months, he would be allowed to have a limited license.

Brad was seizure free for the required six months and was finally able to receive his limited license. No one has ever been more proud than he was of that piece of paper. It wasn't even an official license, but it was a step in that direction. Dave had taken him to the Department of Motor Vehicles for his driving test. He let him drive on the way there, on the freeway of all places. I don't know how they ever made it. After the test, the instructor explained the limitations of Brad's license. He was required to have a licensed driver with him, to drive only during daylight hours, and not to drive on the freeway.

The farthest I could bring myself to let him drive was to the church, two blocks up the street. He had slow reaction times, and I never knew if he would be able to respond quickly enough to unexpected situations. I did plenty of gasping and covering my face just getting to the church.

THINGS TO DO WHILE WAITING FOR THE PHONE TO RING, By Brad Coles, October 13, 1998

1. *Put my clothes in my drawers*
2. *Listen to the radio*
3. *Write a letter to one of my friends*
4. *Go clean the car*
5. *Play basketball with my neighbor*
6. *Play my guitar and practice for my lesson*
7. *Clean my room so my mom doesn't get mad*
8. *Throw out my trash in my room*
9. *Write a novel about myself*
10. *Try to break a piece of wood with my head*
11. *Make a quilt for the winter*
12. *Do my homework*
13. *Find a cure for cancer*
14. *Watch TV for hours*
15. *Sign up to win a million dollars*

Shortly before Christmas of his sophomore year, 1997, he had another CNS relapse. About a week later, just after the beginning of the new year he was hospitalized with a high fever. He stayed only one night, since his blood counts remained at a safe level and his temperature returned to normal.

That relapse and sickness marked the beginning of the end. Somehow I knew this year would be his last. There was no drastic change---just a slowing down of everything he did. Normal activities seemed to require greater effort. He was growing thinner.

Knowing how important it was to Brad, we wanted to make his sixteenth birthday special for him. He had looked forward to it for such a long time. We gave him a party at our house, but he was disappointed that some of his friends didn't show up. Even that couldn't diminish his excitement at being old enough to date and to get his driver's license as soon as he was seizure free for a period of six months.

Brad's first date was the highlight of the school year for him. He was so excited to be going to a school dance on a real date, with a girl that said "yes" to his invitation. He and his date doubled with another couple so that Brad's friend could drive. After dinner and the dance, a group of his friends brought their dates to our house to play games. He was thrilled with how the evening turned out.

Brad's Journal Entry, May 2, 1998

Today was the greatest day in a very very long time. First I went to the Camp Hobe meeting and got to meet all my friends from camp last year. Then I came home and got ready for my date tonight with Julia Robinson to go to the Men's Association Dance. First we went out to dinner at Applebees. Then we went to the dance and got our pictures taken and danced a few times. After that we went to Zucca Juice then came to our house. I had a good time there. Then I dropped her off at her house and if you are wondering, NO, I did not kiss her just yet. Hint Hint.

Brad's Journal Entry, June 3, 1998

Today was the last day of school for my sophomore year. We didn't have to go to classes either. We signed each other's yearbooks and went out to get breakfast. We got our yearbooks last night, so we had most of the signatures already. Tonight we went to Holly's house and went swimming, played games, ate dinner, and watched the Jazz game. It was a great game. They beat the Bulls in overtime 85-88. Well, back to the end of the year. I had a great year and I met a lot of new friends. I became better acquainted with my old friends. It was sad though, seeing it all end again and watching people go their own way. Some good ways, some bad ways, but I hope to see them again one day. I must go now to bed and good night to the class of 1997-1998. It was nice knowing you for the time being. Sincerely to you all with love. Brad Taylor Coles

Chapter 30

SPECIAL FRIENDS

Brad became close friends with the Lewis family who live in our neighborhood. They made him feel like he was part of their family. Julie Lewis was our ward Relief Society president at the time of Brad's first relapse. Later, as Brad was facing the end of his life, her husband, Benson, was a member of our stake presidency. Their friendship went far beyond the duties of their callings. Julie made a hand-tied quilt for Brad from colorful dinosaur print fabric when he had his first relapse. That quilt saw Bradley through many afternoons on the couch, the "barf bucket" nearby. Throughout his life it was his extra cover on cold nights, and a cozy wrap for TV watching. It has now become one of Shane's prize possessions, a tangible fragment of Brad's life that wraps him in memories of his brother.

Julie told me that their family prayed for Brad on a regular basis. I am convinced that those prayers helped to prolong his life and to keep him feeling peaceful. Many good people of various religious beliefs prayed for him over the years, and their collective prayers were heard by a kind Heavenly Father. Including Brad in their family prayers helped the Lewis family feel a special bond with Brad, but it was Shane and Matt, their younger sons, who became his closest buddies.

Brad and Shane Lewis shared a mutual friend, Wendy Bennion. She was one of a group of teens that Brad met at Camp Hobe, who treated Brad like an equal, even though he was seven or eight years younger.

Wendy met Shane Lewis at an EMT class they were both taking through the school district as part of their high school curriculum. Wendy was bald from chemotherapy, but her smile was still beautiful. She was sure she would not be going to prom that year. Who would want to date a bald girl? Shane did. They became very close friends and wrote letters to each other regularly during the two years Shane was in Japan on his mission. Sadly, Wendy's cancer returned. Days before Shane was to return home from Japan, she was so critically ill that he was asked by President Thomas S. Monson of the First Presidency of the LDS Church to come home a few days sooner than planned. President Monson was another person who had been charmed by Wendy's personality. He wanted her to have the wish of seeing her friend again before she died. Shane arrived in time to visit with his friend, and shortly after to speak at her funeral.

I worried about Brad when Wendy died. We had talked with him about how sick she was, and had gone to take her gifts, but I don't know if he thought she would really die. She, like Brad, was one of the survivors; one who beat the odds, who proved the doctors weren't always right in their predictions. Brad had been closer to Wendy than to any other hospital friend that had died. It was a difficult time, but he accepted it pretty well. The church was filled to capacity at her funeral, as hundreds came to remember this beautiful girl with the sparkling eyes and bright smile. I think of Wendy whenever I hear her theme song, "I Believe There Are Angels Among Us." I know there are, and that she is one of them. She and Brad must be having a great time together.

The summer following Wendy's death, Shane Lewis volunteered to be a counselor at Camp Hobe in honor of Wendy's memory and to bring happiness to other kids that had to face the same things that she had suffered. Brad was thrilled to find out that Shane was going to be at camp. A pretty girl named Dixie was also at camp as a girls' counselor.

Brad saw the possibility of romance between Shane and Dixie and set out to make sure the two got together. Shane told Brad that Dixie was cute but was probably too young. Being neither shy nor tactful, Brad asked her how old she was and determined that she was the perfect age for Shane. Brad encouraged their participation in a skit, making sure they had the parts where the guy kisses the girl, and he took pictures. Brad was proud of his success when, after camp, Shane and Dixie began dating.

Some months later, the pair did become engaged. Brad was one of the first friends to whom they told the news. Chances are they would have managed to find romance without Brad's help, but no one could have ever convinced him of that. In his mind they were his own personal success story. He was a handsome and proud young man in his tuxedo on their wedding day as he greeted guests at their reception.

When Bradley started going to Brighton High School as a sophomore he rode the bus, as all of our children had done. Since most of the sophomores ride the bus he actually enjoyed it, meeting Sarah, Trisha and Tara at the bus stop each morning. As the weather got colder though, I began to be concerned about sending him out alone while it was still dark each morning. One day on our way to aerobics class, I mentioned to Julie that I was worried that Brad could have a seizure on the way to the bus stop and freeze out in the snow. She immediately volunteered to have Matt, her youngest son, drive Brad to school. I thanked her and assured her that was not necessary, saying that Dave or I could drive him, and that when there was room, he could ride with Nathan and his friends in their carpool. But Julie insisted that Matt would be happy to drive Brad.

Sure enough, that evening Matt called Brad and told him he would be over before school in the morning. For Brad, this was too cool for words. A popular senior was taking him, a lowly sophomore, to school! Every morning for the rest of the school year Matt was there, sacrificing his own time, gas, and social status to make sure Brad got safely to school.

Brad's Journal Entry, October 15, 1995

Today I got to meet President Monson at church for my friend's (Shane Lewis) missionary homecoming. It was a great experience for me. He kind of knows me now. He was a friend of Wendy Lindsey Bennion who passed away September 29, 1995. She was my bestest and closest friend a person could ever have. I am good friends with her family.

Chapter 31

MIRACLES IN FT. MADISON

1998 was a year of graduations for us. About two weeks after Brad turned sixteen, we drove to Rexburg, Idaho, for Janene's graduation from Ricks College. She received her associate degree in social work, and then moved back home for a few weeks to finish preparations for her wedding in June. She had met Jason Cobia at Ricks the first semester of that year, and they continued a long distance romance after he transferred to BYU in January.

Days after returning from Rexburg, we went to Provo to watch Curtis, our son-in-law, receive his civil engineering degree at BYU. The following month Nathan graduated from Brighton High School and seminary. We went to all four graduations to celebrate the achievements of our children and their spouses.

Curtis had accepted a job in Venezuela. Yes, South America. It was an exciting career opportunity for him as a new graduate, but our family was traumatized at the thought of them moving so far away and taking our first granddaughter, Emily, with them! She was just fifteen months old, and Kristi was expecting their second child in July. He would be born in a foreign country! Even when I reminded Kristi that he would never be able to be president of the United States, they didn't change their minds. Brad, like all of us, had a hard time saying good-bye when we took them to the airport. He and Emily had become good friends over the first year of her life. After Kristi and her family got settled into their new home in Venezuela, an apartment in a high-rise overlooking the Caribbean, we kept in touch through frequent phone calls and chats over the internet.

In early June, two weeks before Janene's wedding, Brad relapsed again. It had been only six months since the previous relapse. Just as the doctors had predicted, the relapses were getting closer together and the drugs seemed to be effective for shorter periods of time.

Kristi and Emily came home at the end of June to attend Janene and Jason's wedding in the Salt Lake Temple. Kristi was just six weeks from the due date of her new baby, and the trip alone with a toddler through foreign airports was very tiring for her. It was wonderful to have them back for a couple of weeks though, and we made the most of every minute. Before they returned to Venezuela, I talked to Kristi about Brad's health and my concern that he wouldn't live much longer. She felt sad about being so far away from the family, but her home was now on another continent with her husband, and she had to go back there.

The day after Kristi and Emily went back to Venezuela, Dave and I and our three boys boarded a flight to Kansas City, on the way to Jason's hometown of Omaha, Nebraska, to attend a reception for him and Janene there. In order to travel to Omaha, we cashed in some of Dave's frequent flier miles for our airline tickets. There were no flights available to Omaha, so we decided to fly into Kansas City and rent a car. We flew out on Tuesday, planning to visit church history sites in that part of the country for a few days before the reception on Friday.

We had a pleasant day on Tuesday, seeing church history sites in the Kansas City area. On Wednesday morning we left early and drove across the state of Missouri to Nauvoo, Illinois. We spent some time there touring the restored village and attending a play. After an evening campfire program, we stopped near the Mississippi River to watch the fireflies, a novelty to us. It was getting late when we started driving west again into Iowa. We didn't have reservations for the night, but planned to drive for a few hours and then find a motel.

The first town we came to was Ft. Madison, Iowa, just across the Mississippi River from Nauvoo. After consulting a map, we realized it might be a long time before we reached another town big enough to have a motel, and all of us were getting tired. We decided it might be best to spend the night in Ft. Madison. The first motel we saw after deciding to stay advertised an indoor pool, a big plus for the boys. The only room available was a smoking room. Normally, I would have chosen to look for another place, but our options seemed limited, and Brad was worn out, so we checked in for the night.

After unloading the car, we went to take a swim before bed. Brad was too tired to swim, so he and I played a short round of miniature golf then went back to the room. Dave soon followed with Nathan and Shane.

Brad got into the shower while Dave started shaving. The other boys and I watched TV in our swimsuits, waiting for our turns in the bathroom. When Brad started talking to himself in the shower, Dave went to check on him. He was not speaking coherently, and Dave wrapped him in a towel and helped him to one of the beds, where he went into a full grand mal seizure. We sat with him, talking to reassure him, expecting the seizure to end in a couple of minutes. It didn't. After maybe ten minutes, I told Nathan to dial 911. I didn't know if there was emergency service of any kind in the area, but we needed to find help. The series of events that followed were miracles: there is no other explanation.

There was a hospital in Ft. Madison, practically next door to our motel. The paramedics arrived in moments after our call. Even in our state of panic and fear we had to laugh at ourselves. We were all dressed only in swimsuits. Dave had shaved half of his face and had shaving cream on the other half. Dave and I grabbed clothes and got dressed, then went to the hospital with Brad, leaving Nathan in charge of Shane. We expected to be back before long.

In the emergency room of the little hospital, Brad was given injections of valium, which relaxed the seizures, but he did not return to consciousness. We gave the doctor a brief medical history, and told him we wanted to contact the oncologists at Primary Children's Hospital to get their input on the best course of action. A nurse made the call, and I was able to talk with a doctor in Salt Lake, who assured me that Brad was getting the same medical care he would have received if he were at home. We discussed his seizure control medication and agreed to give him an extra dose by IV.

Dave and I wanted Brad to receive a priesthood blessing. One of the nurses found a phone book so we could try and find a number for The Church of Jesus Christ of Latter-day Saints. Even though we were only a few miles from Nauvoo, where there are swarms of LDS missionary couples, the local phone book had only the number for the visitors' center there, which was closed for the night. The only other listing we found was for the two young men serving as missionaries in Ft. Madison. We tried to call them and received no answer, since it was past their curfew. The nurses, though, would not give up. They attempted to call the local chapel, to find other numbers for Nauvoo, and then dialed the missionaries' number again. This time they answered.

A nurse brought me the phone after she made the connection, and I explained our situation, asking if they knew any priesthood holder in town that might be able to come and assist Dave in giving Brad a blessing. They didn't, but volunteered to come themselves even though it was past their curfew. They told me they were in bed and would just come in the sweat pants and T-shirts they were wearing. That was fine with me. I was much more concerned about having them come quickly. Soon these two young men arrived at the hospital, not in sweats, but in white shirts and ties, their hair combed. Their mothers would have been proud. I was. They gave our son a beautiful blessing, which gave us hope and comfort.

Brad continued to have seizures. Each time a new one started, he was given another dose of sedatives, causing him to go deeper into unconsciousness. He was admitted to the hospital to spend the night. I called Janene and explained that we would not be in Omaha as soon as planned. We still hoped to leave sometime the next day, as soon as Brad was stable and allowed out of the hospital. It was very late when he finally appeared to be sleeping peacefully. Dave wanted to stay there and I agreed to go back to the motel and stay with Nathan and Shane.

At 2:00 a.m. I had just fallen asleep when the phone rang. Brad was having seizures again. This really scared me. It made no sense that he was not responding to the increased doses of seizure medication and that even with sedatives he was having seizures. At 5:00 a.m. I went back to the hospital. Things were no better.

That day we got a look at modern medicine in a small town hospital. It was amazing. The only neurologist in the region happened to be scheduled to be at Ft. Madison that day, along with a traveling MRI machine. The doctor wanted an EEG done on Brad. He was attached to monitors, just like at home. But instead of someone on the premises reading the test results, they were transmitted by computer directly to Omaha, where qualified personnel read the results.

When it was time for the MRI, Dave and I accompanied Brad down the hall as he was wheeled along in his hospital bed. The seizures were farther apart, but he was not regaining consciousness. Whenever he became coherent enough to talk, he was very scared. He kept saying, “I think I’m going to die. I don't want to die!" It broke my heart. I didn't know what to tell him. He very well might die. I had always prayed that he would have a peaceful end to his life---not like this, in a strange place with seizures racking his body and causing him such fear.

Dave, however, had no hesitation in answering him. "You're not going to die here, Brad. We're going to get you home," he told him over and over. I took Dave aside and asked him how he could say that. He didn't know if Brad was going to die or not. Yes, he assured me. He did know. This was not the way Brad was going to die. Still, I had my doubts.

The nurse and technician took Brad to the end of the hallway with a garage-type door. "We're going outside?" I asked. That, I was told, was where the MRI machine was. The garage door lifted up, and there, sure enough, was the MRI machine, mounted inside the bed of a semi truck.

The technician wanted to sedate Brad even more for the MRI, but I begged him not to. "Please, he has to wake up," I said. "We have to be in Omaha tomorrow night for our daughter's wedding reception. Don't sedate him any more."

Reluctantly, he agreed to try and do the scan without sedation. It was critical for Brad to hold perfectly still so that the image would be clear. I explained to Brad what was going on, and he might have understood, but he was so groggy it was impossible for him to respond. He was eased into the tunnel of the machine, and the noisy scanner roared to life. The noise startled him, and he moved. This happened several times, until the technician was ready to sedate him in spite of my pleading. He decided to attempt holding Brad's chin with his hand during the test. It almost worked. When I realized that it was okay for another person to be in the path of the machine, I told the technician I thought Brad would hold still if I could be the one to hold his head in place. He gave me one last chance. I talked calmly to

Brad and told him how important it was to hold still, that my hand would be holding his face to help him remember.

With me stretched prone across Brad's chest, he was once again eased into the machine. "Please hold still," I whispered. The machine roared to life. Brad held perfectly still. I stretched as far as I could, reassuring him and holding his head in place. The test was a success.

While Brad and I were in the semi truck MRI lab, Dave waited in the hallway of the hospital, since the truck was not large enough for more people. As he waited, he prayed with all his might that the Lord would assist us at this frightening time. Because of his lack of sleep the previous night, Dave fell asleep. After a short time he was awakened by one of the nurses. She had suddenly thought about a close friend of hers who was a member of the LDS faith. She had taken it upon herself to call him and ask that he come over to see if he could be of assistance to this stranded family. Immediately he drove to the hospital. He offered to take care of our kids at the motel or to help in whatever way he could. We were overwhelmed by his generosity in our time of need. Even though we felt we were okay without extra help for the time being, we were touched by the kindness of a stranger and comforted once again that the Lord was watching over us.

As the day wore on, Brad still showed no signs of waking up. I wondered how much of the sleepiness was from the seizures and how much from the medications. The staff at the Ft. Madison Hospital could not have been kinder. Nathan and Shane, tired of the swimming pool at the motel, came over to the hospital. The nurses gave them access to an empty room where they could watch TV and play games. Shane was thrilled with the controls on the hospital bed that he was able to play with. Nathan had been watching TV when a special news bulletin came on. He came to Brad's room and asked if Ft.

Madison was the name of the town we were in. I told him I thought so.

"Well," he said, "there was a train wreck, and parts of Ft. Madison are being evacuated because of toxic fumes." We laughed, thinking our situation just kept getting more complex. The nurses, though, said that we were far enough from the train wreck that we would not be forced to evacuate.

The later it got, the more stressed I became about the fact that we were still many miles from Omaha, about a six-hour drive in fact, and the reception was the next day. The nurses wanted to make sure that at least I would get there, even if Dave had to remain behind with Brad. Without our asking, they checked bus and train schedules and even found someone willing to drive me there! I appreciated their help and suggestions, but I was determined that somehow we were all going together.

We were supposed to have been at Jason's parents' house on Thursday evening, feasting on Omaha steaks. We wished we were. I called Janene again and told her we would do our very best to be at the reception on Friday night. She was disappointed that we were late and might not come at all, but more concerned about Brad, who had been her faithful shadow for so many years.

On Thursday evening I talked to the doctor. Nothing had been determined from the EEG or the MRI, which didn't surprise me. Those same tests had been done on Bradley before with no conclusive results, other than a pattern of brain waves that indicate seizure activity. Brad hadn't had any seizures for several hours, but was still groggy. The doctor agreed that if Brad woke up in the morning, and if his blood tests showed the seizure medication levels to be okay, and if he could walk and eat something, then he would ask the neurologist to release him. Finally, a glimmer of hope.

Friday morning I was at Brad's side, prodding him gently, telling him he needed to wake up so we could go to Janene's reception in Omaha. He was extremely weak and tired, but fully responsive for the first time since the seizures had begun. Dave and I reviewed with him the events of the past two days and asked him if he felt strong enough to leave. Dave was sure it was too soon for him to go anywhere, but Brad said, "I just want to go home."

We propped him up between us and walked him to the shower, cleaned him up, and helped him dress. I called Nathan at the motel and told him to get everything packed and ready to go. Brad forced himself to swallow a bite of food. It was getting later and later in the day. I was almost pacing around, looking at the clock, waiting for blood test results, waiting for the doctor's permission to check out. Finally at about 1:30 p.m. we were on our way, making one quick stop at a drug store for some eardrops for Nathan. He had developed a serious ear infection from his hours of entertaining Shane in the motel swimming pool.

I'm not sure what the speed limit was on the road we took from Ft. Madison to Omaha, but I know Dave exceeded it. I hope he has been forgiven. I phoned Janene along the way, updating her on our progress. I sat in the back seat with Shane and Nathan so that Brad could recline the front seat and rest. At 6:45 p.m. we reached the outskirts of Omaha. At 7:00, the time the reception was starting, we pulled into the Cobia's driveway. They were already at the reception, of course. Dave and I quickly changed clothes. There was no time to find the boys' clothes and iron them, so they remained in the shorts and T-shirts they had been wearing. We were less than half an hour late for the reception.

For most of the evening, Nathan sat with Shane and Brad in a room that we were allowed to use at the hotel. Dave and I enjoyed time with Janene and Jason and his family as we met many of their friends. As it was nearing time for the reception to end, there was a lot of banging on the roof of the reception room. It sounded like construction or heavy furniture being moved upstairs. Then I realized there was a sky light over our heads, and the banging was rain and hail. On the TV the boys were watching, tornado warnings were being posted. Of course, what else? We hadn't had a tornado yet! We still needed to drive three hours to Kansas City that night to catch our flight home in the morning.

When the reception ended, we watched the weather report. The tornadoes seemed to be mainly to the north, and we were going south. As we drove, there was a constant fire works show, lightning touching down around us in every direction and pouring rain. At 1:30 a.m., we arrived at our Kansas City motel and slept for a few hours.

Everything went fine on our flight home the next morning, and Brad didn't have any more seizures. We never could explain why events happened like they did, but we know that the Lord was watching over us. I know we were directed to stay in Ft. Madison, next to the only hospital for miles around, where loving and kind people cared for us. We made it to the reception. And Dave was right: Brad did not die there.

THINGS THAT MAKE YOU NERVOUS, By Brad Coles, November 12, 1998

1. *Not passing classes*
2. *Not passing high school*
3. *Not having friends*
4. *Losing someone close to me*
5. *Dying at a young age*
6. *Not getting my projects done*
7. *Not getting a girl friend*
8. *Not being able to see my sister and her family in Venezuela*
9. *Getting in a car accident*
10. *Not dying a happy man*
11. *Getting another lousy President*
12. *Getting blamed for murder*
13. *Losing my family*
14. *Not having the 49er's make it into Super Bowl 33*
15. *Having another seizure*

Brad and his brothers and sisters at the Salt Lake Temple for Janene's wedding, June 1998 (Left to right: Kristi, Nathan, Shane, Janene, Brad, Alisa)

Chapter 32

STILL HAVE MY GOOD LOOKS

Brad was excited to be starting his junior year of high school. He was actually glad to be back in the routine of school where he could see his friends every day. Most of them now had jobs, so they had not been available as often during the summer to "hang out." Brad wanted so badly to have a job himself. He wanted to earn money as his sisters and Nathan had done, to pay for dates and clothes and to have some cash in his pocket. I tried to think of some kind of work he might be able to do, but there was nothing that sounded feasible. He was so tired all the time now.

Every day after school he rested on the family room couch. Nathan had moved to Provo to attend BYU, and Brad and Shane were the only kids left at home. Brad got home from school about half an hour before Shane, so he had some quiet time every afternoon. When Shane got home they often played video games together.

Brad's Journal Entry, September 5, 1998

Today was pretty good. I woke up and went fishing with my family. Nate brought some of his college friends with us. We caught a lot of fish but could only keep three of them because the others were too small. It started to rain while we were there, so we left. We went to Swiss Days on the way home and

Shane and I got rubber band guns. BYU lost their game today, but not by much. Well, it's time to get some beauty sleep, so goodnight y'all.

Kristi and Curtis were anxious to have us come and visit them in Venezuela. Their baby, Matthew, had been born July 23, and we had not seen him yet. I convinced Dave that he and I should go in October. Brad and Shane begged to go with us, but I told them it was too expensive. Since we were using frequent flyer miles for our tickets, that wasn't the main reason. It was just too risky to take Brad out of the country. After our experiences in Ft. Madison, Iowa, it was obvious he could have unexpected medical complications at any time. Having him in a hospital in Venezuela was an experience we wanted to avoid. Dave thought we should wait until the first of the year to go. Somehow I knew that Brad would be too sick then. We needed to make the trip while he was still well enough to stay home without us. I'm not sure how I knew that, but I did.

This was another time the choices we faced were difficult. Brad's health was failing, and a week away from him was one less week that we would be able to enjoy time with him. But Kristi and her family were also important to us, as was meeting our new grandson. We needed to go. Kristi was feeling pretty isolated from our family and wanted us to come and see the sights of Venezuela, and especially Matthew. She and Curtis decided to wait until we were there to give Matthew a name and a blessing. Curtis' parents were living in Caracas, Venezuela, at that time, about a three-hour drive away from Kristi and Curtis in Puerto La Cruz. They were planning to come for the blessing as well. When we told my parents about our plans, they volunteered to come to Utah and take care of Brad and Shane while we were gone.

Dave and I had a wonderful time in Venezuela, in spite of the fact that Dave was nervous the whole time we were there, since he could not understand Spanish and did not know what anyone was saying. We played with Emily, got acquainted with Matt, and went swimming and snorkeling in the transparent blue Caribbean.

The day after we returned from our trip, Brad showed me a painful rash that had started to develop on his arms and legs. It was unlike anything I had seen, so we went to the hospital where it was determined that he had shingles. As much as I had enjoyed the trip, I knew it was now time for me to be home with Brad. I was grateful that the rash had not become a problem while we were gone.

Through the rest of October and into November, things were pretty uneventful. Brad and Shane went to school; we did activities on most weekends with Nathan, Alisa and Steven, and Janene and Jason. I began Christmas shopping. Once a week Brad and I went to the hospital. His blood counts were low, but safe enough for him to get chemotherapy most of the time. Brad went to football games and parties whenever he had the energy. But more and more he opted to stay home and watch videos or play games with Shane.

We enjoyed Thanksgiving with our family, having all of our children except Kristi's family come for the day. Alisa was now expecting her second child, and Janene her first, so we had two more grandchildren to look forward to. Brad lacked the energy to play in our ward's annual Turkey Bowl football game on Thanksgiving morning, but he still wanted to be involved in the activity. Dave let him take the go-cart up to the school where the game was being played. He gave rides around the parking lot to all the little kids that were there.

THINGS THAT I'M THANKFUL FOR, By Brad Coles, November 19, 1998

1. *A great place to live*
2. *Some really good friends*
3. *My great family I have*
4. *My really cool guitar*
5. *Just being alive*
6. *My really cool stereo*
7. *Living in a free country*
8. *My new nephew*
9. *My go-cart*
10. *Having breaks from school*
11. *Still having my good looks*
12. *Not being in the slums*
13. *Having all the food I can eat*
14. *Going snow mobiling every February*
15. *Snowy mountains to go skiing down*

Brad's Journal Entry, November 26, 1998

Today was Thanksgiving. It was pretty good. We had the Turkey Bowl but I didn't feel good enough to play, so I brought up the go-cart and played on it. Janene, Jason, and his sister came to our house for dinner. We all had a great time together. We played games and ate a lot of food. We also watched a lot of football on TV. Then Steven and Alisa showed up to stay overnight and go shopping in the morning. We also started to watch a lot of Christmas movies tonight. Well, time for some sleep.

With the start of December, Brad began to have headaches almost constantly. A spinal tap did not show an abnormal number of blast cells, so he took Tylenol, had a nap after school every day, and kept going. If there was anything Brad was looking forward to as much as Christmas itself, it was the high school Christmas dance. He had invited Lindsey, a girl in our neighborhood who was actually shorter than he was. A group of his friends planned to attend the dance together.

The first week of December his blood counts were too low for chemotherapy. The second week they were too low again. I found myself counting the days until the dance, hoping and praying that he would be well enough to go.

On the day of the dance he felt weak and exhausted. His head hurt, but he never even considered canceling his plans. Much of the day he rested, but by evening he was dressed up, hair carefully combed, and ready to go. He and Lindsey, as well as the others in their group, had a great time. It was his last date.

Brad's Journal Entry, December 5, 1998 (his last journal entry)

Today I spent the day with my family. We went to the hospital Christmas party and then we went to the Festival of Trees. It was pretty fun. We went through the malls downtown and came home. I took a long nap and then later on that night I had my friends over to hang out and watch the movie "Dr. Doolittle." It was pretty good. I laughed through most of the movie. After the movie was done we pretty much told jokes and laughed at them. Well, I must get some sleep now.
P.S. Twenty days left until Christmas

Group picture from the Christmas Dance, 1998 (Lindsey and Brad are seated on the far left)

Chapter 33

YOU REALIZE THIS IS SERIOUS

As I did Brad's Christmas shopping, I had a feeling that he would not be using his gifts for long. That Christmas 1998, we had just our three boys at home. Our daughters were spending the holiday with their in-laws. I felt it would be Brad's last Christmas, and I knew that it would be the last Christmas before Nathan's church missionary service would take him away from home for two years. In the back of my mind was the thought that the following year Shane would be the only child left at home. We had a wonderful morning with our boys. Alisa and her family came later in the day to have dinner with us. On Christmas night my parents arrived to spend a few days.

The day after Christmas we went bowling with my parents, our boys, and Alisa's family. Brad, never one to complain, did his best to bowl. He was so weak that one time, as he attempted to throw the ball, he lost his balance and fell. I tried to ignore the sick feeling I experienced when I realized just how little strength he had. He laughed at himself, got up, and finished the game.

BRAD'S CHRISTMAS WISH LIST, 1998

Play Station or Nintendo 64
New headphone set
All of Garth Brooks new C.D.'s or the Limited Series
Zorro, the movie
NSYNC C.D.
Game Boy Color
Punching bag or workout set
Computer game Top Gun, and Disney Magic Artist
A banana chair with a massager
New camera
Remote control car
Turn my room into a 49er's room
Utah edition Monopoly

On the Monday following Christmas, Brad was scheduled to have a spinal tap and a bone marrow aspiration to determine the cause of his consistently low blood counts. We hoped by doing the tests we could rule out a relapse, but I was not overly optimistic. I expected blast cells would be found in his spinal fluid indicating another central nervous system relapse. That would explain the fact that he had been having headaches.

The procedures were done in the outpatient surgery area rather than in the oncology clinic, since Brad wanted to be put to sleep. He had endured countless bone marrow aspirations and spinal taps without anesthesia, but that day he did not feel well enough to deal with the pain.

After Brad woke up from the anesthesia, Dave and I went downstairs with him to await results of the tests. I didn't feel too concerned until the medical personnel started to assemble in our room. Dr. Roberts came in first. Then came another doctor, a nurse, and a second nurse. By now I was more than a little nervous. A child life specialist was followed by a social worker. Oh no, not a social worker! The news was going to be bad, bad, bad. When there had been previous relapses, the most we had met with was two doctors, or a doctor and a nurse, or even just one doctor. After all, we were veterans, accustomed to trauma, immune to fear. Ha! Not now. Not with the grim-faced group in this examining room.

Brad hardly glanced up. He concentrated on his video game, ignoring the others. This was it. For fourteen years we had known this day might come, and now it was here. It seemed all the oxygen had been sucked out of the room as I attempted to breathe normally. Dr. Roberts started to speak. I knew the words before they came out of his mouth. Relapse. Not just the central nervous system, which I had suspected, but the bone marrow as well. A death sentence; no one had to say it. After fourteen years and about a dozen relapses, we knew.

"You realize this is serious, that you will have to make some hard choices?"

"Brad, you know this is serious, don't you?"

He nodded and played on. This was very unusual. He showed no emotion and asked no questions about having his medications increased. He knew what the relapse meant and there was nothing he or any of us could do. We had tried all the conventional treatments known since the time of his diagnosis at age two. He had responded well, but not well enough. Now the drugs were losing and the leukemia was winning.

One doctor held out hope. Dr. Bowens told us about a clinical trial, very early stage, of a substance called B-pap. It was being used experimentally with some apparent success. A glimmer of hope came back. He would beat it again! He had fooled everyone before, and now he would be part of a medical break-through, a cure at last for childhood leukemia. It was worth a try.

Even if it didn't cure our son, maybe the information gained could benefit someone else. Brad listened to what the doctors had to say and agreed to try the B-Pap treatment.

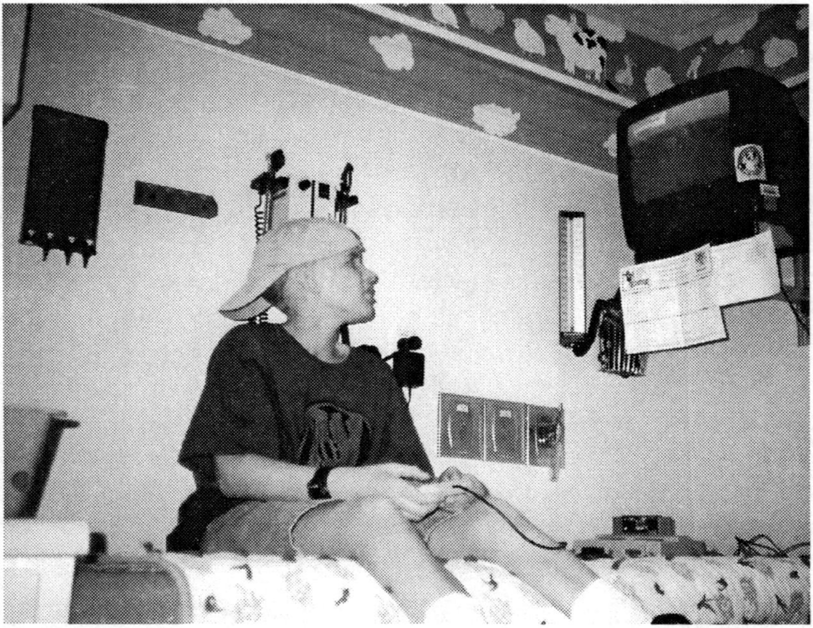

Brad playing video games in the treatment room at Primary Children's Hospital, 1998

Chapter 34

HOW COULD WE LET HIM GO?

It was only three days after Christmas when we heard the dreaded diagnosis of double relapse. Brad was not admitted to the hospital that afternoon. None of the doctors felt there was any value in giving him more chemotherapy. They talked about "comfort measures" and "quality of life" for whatever length of time he had left.

We took Brad home and set about the task of notifying our family about the relapse, never a pleasant task, and now more difficult than ever before. My parents were still in town, so we told them in person rather than over the phone. I always felt bad calling Dave's parents about new problems with Brad. Dave's brother Paul had developed testicular cancer at age eighteen and died a year and a half later. Our experiences with Brad recalled painful memories for them of losing their own young son.

Telling our children was the worst of all. We had all known for fourteen years this time could come, although we had prayed it would not. Many miracles had postponed it for a remarkably long time. How could we deal with it? I was glad our daughters were married and had their husbands to help them through this time. Nathan, however, was facing this trauma on his own, which concerned Dave and me. He was living with roommates that were not even aware that Brad had cancer. He was preparing to start a new semester of school, anticipating a two-year church mission the next summer, and facing losing his little brother.

We told everyone who really needed to know about the relapse, and then I tried to read and understand the stack of paperwork for the clinical trial of B-Pap that we had decided to pursue. Brad was tired and went to bed early. When I went up to get ready for bed a couple of hours later, he called to me and said he didn't feel well.

I went into his room and felt his forehead. Hot! Not just feverish, but burning hot. I pulled off his covers, got a cool cloth for his face, and took his temperature. It was 105.7 degrees Fahrenheit. I started to cry. He might die this very night! A call to the hospital confirmed that we had no choice but to admit him. Dave insisted on taking him to the hospital himself, telling me to stay home and get some sleep. I did stay home, but I didn't sleep much.

The next morning my parents returned home to California. My mom offered to stay and take care of Shane. I told her we would be okay since Nathan was still at home for the rest of his Christmas break, and no one knew what to expect with Brad's situation. His fever had dropped considerably with the aid of the IV antibiotics he received during the night, and he felt reasonably well.

Dr. Bowens had ordered the B-Pap, and Brad received his first dose that day. I was shocked to see two nurses come into his hospital room in full protective covering from head to toe to inject the medication into his IV line.

"Is it really that toxic?" I wanted to know.

"Well," one nurse replied, "it's like giving chemotherapy. We don't want to get any on us. Don't the nurses in the clinic always wear protective gear to give chemotherapy?"

"No, I've never seen such a thing." Suddenly I appreciated more than ever all the oncology staff and the risks they faced every day in treating childhood cancer patients in as kind and humane a way as possible. They chose to skip the protective covering that made them look like space creatures in order to avoid scaring the children.

The phlebotomist came the morning following the first dose of B-Pap to draw some of Brad's blood. Dave and I waited anxiously for the results, hoping for an indication that the experimental drug was at work destroying leukemia cells. There was no improvement. Ever the optimist, Dr. Bowens assured us that the results might not come until after the second dose. The second dose was given, then a few days later the third and final dose. Still no change. The drug had done nothing to improve Brad's blood counts. We were out of options. Now even Dr. Bowens had no choice but to have a talk with Dave and me about how best to care for Brad during his final weeks or days.

The two of us met with him privately in a conference room of the hospital. We wanted to know what to expect and how to best help Brad. The doctor was factual with us about the ways a person with leukemia might die. In Brad's case, a seizure could kill him. If his blood platelets were too low, he could die of a hemorrhage. He would probably experience excruciating bone pain as the leukemia cells built up in his bone marrow and put pressure from the inside on every bone in his body. The good news was that he could be given morphine in whatever doses were required to control the pain.

As New Year's Eve approached, Brad was disappointed to be spending it at the hospital, knowing that his friends were going out to parties without him. Some of them called that evening to wish him a Happy New Year. Our family had started a tradition years before of having appetizers for dinner on New Year's Eve. Obviously that could not happen this year.

Nathan planned to bring Shane to the hospital and visit awhile before going out with his friends. He surprised us by bringing a complete New Year's Eve party to the hospital for Brad. He had made several of our favorite recipes. We had a great time together, eating and laughing, wishing each other a Happy New Year a few hours early. By the time Nathan left, Brad was ready to go to sleep. Before I took Shane home, I stood at the window and looked out at the lights of the city below. At midnight it would be 1999, nearly the end of the century, and even nearer the end of Brad's life.

When Nathan returned to BYU for the beginning of winter semester, taking care of Shane became more complicated. He was nine, too young to be alone, especially at such a difficult time. Fortunately, Dave's employer was very supportive, allowing him to miss planned business trips and spend as much time as necessary at the hospital with Brad.

Each of the next few mornings I got Shane ready for school then went to an aerobics class before going to the hospital. It seemed rather selfish to take an hour for myself, but I needed the physical and emotional outlet before facing another day at the hospital. Dave stayed with Brad until I arrived, then went to work until about 3:00 p.m. He returned to the hospital so I could go home at the time Shane was finished with school. I did household chores, helped Shane with homework and fixed him dinner, then took him with me to the hospital. Dave would then take Shane home, eat his dinner, shower and get clean clothes, and come back to the hospital at around nine or ten o'clock to spend the night, while Shane and I went home to sleep.

Brad was concerned when school started that he would get behind in his classes. No one knew if he would ever be well enough to go back to school, but it was important to him to feel like he was still part of the world of high school where his friends were. I contacted the school about their home and hospital program, but they didn't feel Brad fit the criteria since I could not tell them how long he would be out of school. Finally I talked to one of Brad's teachers, who was also a family friend, about the difficulty I was having working with the school. She said that she would be his personal teacher and take care of anything that needed to be done with the school. It was a great relief to both Brad and me, even though he never got well enough to do any more schoolwork.

Throughout his stay in the hospital, Brad continued to receive visits and phone calls from his friends. One day when Trisha, Sarah, Tara, and Laura were visiting at the hospital, Brad felt well enough to walk down to the game room with them. Here was this skinny little guy shuffling along with his IV pole, surrounded by four attractive girls. Another teenage boy saw them and asked, “Are those your sisters or something?”

“No,” Brad replied with obvious pride. “These are my friends.” He was always happiest when surrounded by a group of nice-looking girls.

On the tenth of January the doctors decided Brad was well enough to be released from the hospital. He continued to receive IV antibiotics at home. For the next four days he and Shane played with their new Christmas video games. He slept in his own bed, snuggled under his new 49er’s throw. He was not well enough to attend school, but he kept in contact with his friends through phone calls.

On Thursday, January 14, Brad was scheduled to return to the clinic at the hospital for blood tests. After Shane went to school I took Brad to the clinic. Dave was in Baltimore, Maryland, on a business trip.

Because he was so frail, and there was snow and ice in patches on the ground to make walking hazardous, I drove Brad up to the door of the hospital and let him out before I went to park the car. As I watched him go in through the door, I was shocked to see that he was shuffling along without really picking up his feet. His heel came up slightly; he slipped his foot forward, and then repeated the action with his other leg, his toes never completely leaving the ground.

After having his blood drawn, he went to an examining room to wait his turn to see a doctor. The exam went well, and he had no new complaints about how he was feeling. As Brad was putting on his shoes and we were preparing to go home, Sarah, his nurse, came in with some bad news. His blood test had shown that he had a staph infection. He needed to be readmitted to the hospital for immediate treatment.

Alisa agreed to bring Katie and stay at our house with Shane that night, even though she was in her eighth month of pregnancy. As soon as Brad was admitted and settled into a room upstairs on the third floor, I left him for a short time so I could go home to be with Shane until Alisa arrived and to get some clothes for Brad and me.

On Friday, as soon as he got back into town, Dave came straight from the airport to the hospital. He and I met with Dr. Bowens again, who told us to prepare for Brad's death in whatever ways we could. We relied strongly on our faith and our unfailing belief that the Lord was in charge of Brad. Still, I didn't know how I could ever possibly let him go.

That evening, all of our children except Kristi came to visit Brad. Several friends also came by to see him. We had been in frequent contact with Kristi by phone, and she kept asking when she should come. There was no way to know. She needed to travel alone with two babies from South America. How could we time her trip so that she could see Bradley alive and not need to make a second trip for his funeral, or spend a long time away from Curtis?

It was a sad evening that we spent together. When our children got ready to leave, Dave and I walked them out so we could discuss Brad's condition. As I left, I told Brad we would be right back.

"Okay," he said. "Don't worry. If I die, I die."

It shocked me that he was so blunt. But then I recognized that he had accepted his fate. He was at peace, unlike the experience at Ft. Madison, when he had been terrified of death.

Dave and I talked briefly with our other children, letting them know the latest updates from the doctors and what we knew of how and when Brad's life might end. With tears and heavy hearts, Alisa and Steven and Janene and Jason returned to their homes in Provo. Nathan, who was spending the weekend at home, took Shane to our house. After Brad was settled for the night, I went home also.

A short time later Brad called to tell me good night. As we talked, he suddenly began to cry. He seemed overcome by the realization that he was really going to loose the battle this time, and might not ever talk with me again. He was too upset to finish the conversation.

That night as I prayed, I believe I came to know the literal feeling of a broken heart. The anguish I experienced as I contemplated life without Brad, caused me physical pain deep inside. I would have to walk past his room each day, knowing he would never be there again. Never again would I hear him come banging in the door after school calling out, "Hey Mom, I'm home!" The more I thought of situations when I was going to miss him, the harder it was to bear the pain. Finally, I fell into bed and into an exhausted sleep.

About five in the morning on Saturday the phone rang. Dave told me that Brad's temperature was over 105 degrees again. The nurses had been trying for a while to cool him down, but his fever was still climbing higher. The ringing phone also woke up Nathan, who came to my room to see what was wrong. He wanted to go with me to the hospital, but finally agreed to stay with Shane so we would not need to wake him up so early. I promised to call as soon as I got there and let him know if Brad was getting worse.

By the time I got to the hospital, Brad's temperature had begun to decrease. It never got all the way down to a normal reading, but it was out of the danger zone. Dave and I both spent the day at the hospital. In the late afternoon, Nathan and Shane came back to visit. Nathan teased and tickled Brad until he laughed. It was wonderful for all of us to hear that famous giggle one more time. Some other friends and his cousin, Mark, came to visit in the evening.

As the last visitors began to trickle out, Brad was exhausted from all the activity. I was talking to him when I saw his eyes roll back in his head, and I knew he was having a seizure. Immediately, Dave called to a nurse that it was an emergency, and she came rushing in along with Dr. Bowens.

"He needs Valium!" I instructed, only afterward being a little embarrassed at telling the doctor what to do. He agreed, and almost immediately the valium was added to Brad's IV line. His seizure stopped. Brad was still alive.

"Heavenly Father," I prayed silently, "please don't let him die like that. Don't let him bleed to death, or end in a violent seizure. Please let him go peacefully."

Brad slowly regained consciousness, but he was unable to speak clearly. Dave and I both stayed until he seemed stabilized, then Dave insisted that I go home for the rest of the night. Even with Nathan home, Shane still needed me, and I knew I should try and get some sleep to help me face whatever was ahead.

Chapter 35

BUTTERFLIES

The phone rang early Sunday morning.

"You'd better come. He's starting to see things in the room," Dave told me in a calm voice.

"What kinds of things?"

"Butterflies. He says they're all over the room. Hurry. I don't think he's going to be with us much longer."

Taking a deep breath, I tried to make sense out of what was happening. "Dave, I don't think I can do this."

"Yes, you can. We both can."

I threw on some clothes and let Nathan know he was in charge of Shane again. I didn't take time for make-up or combing my hair. Backing the car out of the driveway, I forced the cold engine to accelerate as I headed down the street in the frigid January pre-dawn.

During the drive to the hospital on the deserted freeway, I tried to prepare myself for Brad's death. I was still afraid of how it might happen. I remembered a quote by someone that said, "It's not being dead I'm afraid of. It's getting dead that bothers me."

Throughout all his treatments Dave or I had been with Brad. We had held his hand during bone marrow aspirations and spinal taps. We sat through MRI's, CAT scans, EEG's, echocardiograms, x-rays, and radiation treatments. We had held "barf buckets" and paced the floor of hospital rooms. Through two surgical procedures and hundreds and hundreds of blood tests we had been there.

We could not be with him through the door of death. We could stay with him until he reached it, but then he would have to continue on without us. I didn't know how to die. There was no advice I could give him. I thought back to the promise given to Brad several years previous in a priesthood blessing he received from Elder Loren C. Dunn, a member of the First Quorum of the Seventy of the LDS Church. The only words I could remember from that blessing were: "No matter what you have to go through, you'll never be alone." I knew that someone was going to be with Brad as he passed through that door without us.

Arriving at the hospital, I hurried up to the third floor. At that time Brad was in a room just off the main entry. I could see him as I crossed the hallway. The head of his bed was elevated, and he was smiling, a smile that glowed from somewhere deep inside him. I sat down on the edge of his bed and said, "So, Brad. Dad tells me you have been seeing butterflies."

He nodded and grinned, a look of wonder on his face. He tried to tell me some of what he had described to his dad, but the words were hard for him to form and he let Dave tell me the following story while he smiled in agreement:

Brad had been sleeping fitfully and running a fever most of the night. He had not recovered strength or the ability to communicate fluently after the seizure on Friday evening. When he awoke about five o'clock Sunday morning, the nurse gave him some medication to lower his temperature that also seemed to help him go back to sleep. A little before six o'clock he suddenly woke up, began looking around the room, and grinning. Dave asked, "What is it, Brad?"

"Dad, there are butterflies all over the room! Hundreds of them!" He was wide-awake but spoke softly, and Dave had to lean very close to hear him. Assuming he was seeing into the next world, Dave asked Brad if he saw anything else. At the same time he picked up the phone to call me at home.

"There are trees and plants and animals. It's just like being at the zoo. And there's a little girl. She's playing." Then he asked, "Dad, can I go?"

Dave, without hesitation replied, "No, Brad, not yet. Kristi is coming to see you with Emily and Matthew. Will you wait until they come?"

Brad nodded and relaxed. Then he said in a tired voice, "Dad, can you make the butterflies go away now?"

By the time I reached the hospital, Brad was thoroughly back in our world, but had an expression of pure joy on his face unlike anything I have ever seen. When I looked into his eyes I saw into him, past the physical surface into a space that was both wonderful and disconcerting. I couldn't look for very long.

I have no proof that Brad was looking into the next world. I don't need any. Whatever he saw made him happier than anything this earth has to compare with, and that gives me overwhelming peace. In our family, butterflies will forever remind us of Brad and keep him a part of our lives.

Later that morning we called Kristi to tell her Brad was getting near the end. I let Brad talk to her on the phone and that conversation must have convinced her it was time for her to come. Brad was cheerful, but his speech was slow and slurred. He had difficulty thinking of the words to say and had to make an effort to talk. Kristi told us she was going to buy airline tickets for her and the children to come on the soonest flight possible. She made the plans and called back to tell us they would arrive on Monday afternoon.

By Monday morning Brad was worsening considerably. He struggled to speak. Standing, even with help, was almost impossible for him. His muscles were losing strength. All day Dave and I watched the clock, waiting anxiously for Kristi's flight to arrive, praying she would get there in time to see her little brother alive and to let him see her and the children. Brad mostly slept. Every time he dozed off, I wondered if he would wake up again. He had lost interest in food. When his meals arrived, I tried to spoon in a few bites of food, and he dutifully attempted to eat. The only food that seemed to taste good to him were the miniature cheese-filled cracker sandwiches that we got for him from the snack cart. He put one in his mouth and then began to chew very, very slowly. Swallowing was becoming too big of an effort. After a few minutes, he was done eating and went back to sleep.

At last it was time for Dave to go to the airport and pick up Kristi and her children. As soon as they retrieved their luggage, they came directly to the hospital. I felt a huge sense of relief at their arrival. All of our children could now be together, at least for a short time. When Kristi walked in with Emily and Matthew, Brad broke into a huge grin. He reached out to hold Emily. Thank goodness she is an outgoing child, or the strange hospital environment and the sight of her very sick uncle would have frightened her. After only a moment's hesitation Emily threw her arms around him in a big bear hug. Brad was happy to see her and to finally meet Matthew. Brad was too weak to hold Matthew, so Kristi held him on Brad's lap while they got acquainted.

They visited awhile, but they were all exhausted from their long trip, and Kristi left to take them to our house and get some rest. Later that night as I was getting ready to go home, Brad said something to me that I couldn't hear. His voice was so weak that I had to put my ear next to his mouth while he repeated what he had said.

"Mom, everything is easier now." I repeated it back to make sure I had heard correctly. He smiled and nodded, then relaxed and immediately fell asleep. I didn't know if he would ever wake up again. He had waited for

Kristi to come, as he had agreed, but now he could let go of this life at any time. I wanted to stay the night, but Dave promised to call if anything changed. I agreed to go home and visit with Kristi and Emily and Matthew. I needed to give Kristi instructions about Shane's schedule, since she would be taking care of him now.

Kristi's Account of Her Trip to Utah

On January 17, 1999, Brad woke up in the morning and butterflies were in the room with him. Later that day, Dad called me in Venezuela and told me Brad wasn't going to be here much longer. It didn't take me long to decide that I needed to come up if I wanted a chance to say good-bye. Curtis was still in bishopric meeting at church, and I called him on his cell phone and interrupted his meeting to tell him he needed to come home right away. That was about 5:00 p.m. We packed everything for Emily, Matthew and me and got ready to leave for Caracas.

It took us four and a half hours to drive to Caracas that night because one of our headlights burned out on the way. The roads between Puerto La Cruz and Caracas were not lit at all and were not marked very well for driving at night under the best of circumstances. But we followed close behind one car nearly all the way there and used their lights as our own. We arrived (at Curtis' parent' home) in Caracas at about 1:00 a.m. and had to leave for the airport at 5:00 a.m. We got checked in at the counter, and went through the security gates. They only allow ticketed passengers, so Curtis could not go with me. We were almost on the plane when a customs worker stopped me and wanted Matthew's Venezuelan passport.

We had no idea that he needed a Venezuelan passport. He had his American passport, he is an American citizen, and has American parents. We didn't know that we had missed a step. Before a child born in Venezuela can leave the country, he or she had to have a Venezuelan passport. I was so confused by his Spanish that he allowed Curtis to come and talk to him. I understood little of what was being said, but it seemed to me that they didn't want to let Matthew out of the country. I got so flustered that I finally mustered up my best Spanish and proceeded to yell at the man that I didn't care what he said, but I was taking my son and leaving the country and that was final!

I tried to explain that it was an emergency and that I needed to leave right away. He didn't seem to care too much. After Curtis calmed me down and said a few more convincing words, the man let us go ahead. Later Curtis explained to me that the man probably just wanted money before letting Matthew out of the country, but Curtis wasn't willing to give him any. We were really lucky that he let Matt go at all. It was a frustrating start to the long day ahead of me, traveling alone with two kids.

In Utah we went straight from the airport to the hospital. It was really a shock for me to see Bradley. I hadn't seen him in almost seven months, and he didn't even look like the same person. I was overwhelmed at first, but then Brad smiled at us, and somehow his smile just lit up the room and made everything okay. Brad was so excited to see Emily and Matthew. Emily gave Brad a big hug. She had missed him so much! I remember putting Matthew carefully in Brad's arms. I will never forget the look on Brad's face as he held his nephew for the first and last time.

It was late when I finally got home and went to bed. I kept expecting to have sleepless nights, but thankfully I was sleeping well, probably from exhaustion. I had been asleep for a few hours, when I suddenly woke up knowing the answer to a question that had been troubling me. I had wanted to know who would be with Bradley after he died and I had to stay behind. Both my parents and Dave's were still living. The only people Brad had known personally that had passed away were his friends from Camp Hobe and from the hospital. It seemed reasonable that he would see them, but they were not family.

Now I knew who would be with him. It was my grandpa, Wendell Perkins. I had seen his face in my mind and was given the strong message that he was going to take care of Brad for me. I lay on my back, thinking that it made perfect sense. Grandpa was one of my favorite people. I felt a tremendous sense of relief realizing that I could trust Brad to his care, and he truly would not be alone.

Tuesday morning, as soon as Shane was off to school, Kristi and I took her kids to stay with her sister-in-law who lived nearby, then we went back to the hospital. As we drove, she commented that the next Sunday would be Emily's second birthday, and she hoped Brad wouldn't die that day. I had already thought of that myself. It would be sad for Emily to be reminded every year that her uncle died on her birthday. I told Kristi it was unlikely to happen, since I didn't think he would live that long.

Dave chose to stay at the hospital that day rather than go to work. In the afternoon, I left Kristi at the hospital and went home to be with Shane after school and to pick up Emily and Matthew from their aunt's house. Since Kristi had been away for so long, I wanted to give her a chance to spend time with Brad for a few hours. I did not anticipate how difficult it would be for me to leave him. As much as I enjoyed seeing my grandchildren after months of being apart, I knew I needed to be back at the hospital.

Matthew and Emily were ready for naps, so I put Matthew in the crib and Emily on Shane's bed then went to help Shane with his homework. After a short time, when it sounded like they had gone to sleep, I sent

Shane to check on them. He returned laughing, and said, "Mom, you've got to come see this."

We went upstairs to his room where Emily was lying on the floor, fast asleep, surrounded by candy wrappers and holding a whole, uneaten candy bar in her hand. It seems she had snooped in Shane's drawers and found his private candy stash, then fallen asleep before taking even one bite. I got the camera and took a picture before sliding the candy bar out of her hand and covering her with a blanket.

Back at the hospital, Dave had left Kristi with Brad, saying he was going to the cafeteria for something to eat. He had been gone for quite a long time, and Kristi was starting to be concerned about him. During this same time our stake president, Dean Kennington, came to Brad's hospital room. He seemed surprised to find neither Dave nor I there, since he had felt impressed to come and visit us. He had canceled previous appointments for the evening and called his counselor, Benson Lewis, to meet him at the hospital. Kristi offered to go find her dad. After a fruitless search of the cafeteria, she had a feeling where she might find him.

Opening the door of the little chapel down the hall from Brad's room, she saw Dave kneeling beside the sofa, where he had been praying for guidance, when he had dozed off. We were agonizing over some major decisions about Brad's care, and the answer to Dave's prayer for help came in the form of President Kennington. Dave called home and asked me to come as quickly as I could.

This meant I had to find baby-sitters, at dinnertime, for Emily and Matthew as well as Shane. Fortunately, Kristi's sister-in-law was willing to baby-sit Emily and Matthew again. Shane could have gone there with them, but I felt he would be happier with the family of one of his friends.

It took three phone calls before I was able to find a friend who could watch Shane. That friend, Kathy

Oldroyd, was more than willing to help. I was touched by her response. She had been wondering what she could do to help us. Could she fix Shane dinner? Would he like to spend the night? What else did we need? Please, call whenever you need anything. This experience taught me an important lesson: remember to respond in the same manner when others need my help.

When I finally got to the hospital, both President Kennington and President Lewis were waiting with Dave in the chapel. Kristi joined us there as they gave Dave and me priesthood blessings of comfort and peace. They stayed and counseled with us about our concerns, reassuring us that the Lord knew Brad, and us, and would help us through the challenges we faced.

That night I did not go home. After being away from Brad during the afternoon, I knew I would be worried about him every minute I was away. Kristi took over with the responsibilities at home so I could concentrate on Brad.

Brad, at age 16

Chapter 36

THE JOY WAS GONE

One of the decisions Dave and I had to make was whether to take Brad home or keep him at the hospital. Because Brad had spent so much time at the hospital he was very comfortable there. Every time he was concerned about his health, he had always wanted to go to the hospital, where he knew he would be well cared for. There were some advantages to being at home, but Dave and I both felt it was wiser to stay at the hospital where immediate medical help was available for Brad's needs around the clock.

Once our decision had been made to stay, the hospital staff made arrangements to move Brad to a more private room at the end of a hallway. By the time he was taken there on Wednesday, he was experiencing bone pain. When he had to be touched in any way, he cried in pain. Dr. Bowens explained the morphine pump, which was added to Brad's IV line. We were able to turn up the dose for him as needed. The problem was, he was not verbally responsive, so we had to guess how much medication was necessary to keep him comfortable. He was slipping deeper and deeper into an unreachable state. He could not talk and responded to questions by only a weak squeeze of our hands. We were now praying that he would be released from his pain soon. I did not want him to die, but anything was better than watching him suffer.

Since Brad could no longer get up to use the bathroom, it was necessary for him to get a catheter. I assumed the procedure would be done by one of the regular nurses, so it was a wonderful surprise when Irish, a male nurse who was one of Brad's good friends from Camp Hobe, came instead. I knew Brad was being cared for by someone he loved and trusted. I left the room to spare Brad a little dignity and to spare myself the trauma of watching him endure even more pain. As I reentered the room after the procedure, big, strong Irish was sitting in the rocking chair, holding Brad across his lap like a small child while another nurse changed the bedding. He had tears in his eyes.

The bed was fitted with a special air mattress designed to reduce bedsores. We had been trying to reposition Brad slightly every few hours by propping pillows around him, but no matter how carefully and gradually he was moved, he cried out, as every bone in his body was now filled with pressure from the multiplying leukemia cells. Irish, fighting his own tears at his little friend's pain, gently set him back onto the bed. We kept the foam pad, which had previously been on the bed for Dave to use on the floor as his bed since both of us were staying at the hospital twenty-four hours a day. I slept on the fold-out cot provided for parents.

An unexpected advantage to being at the hospital was privacy. Unlike those previous weeks when we had welcomed all of Brad's friends, who came frequently, we now wanted to have this time alone with family members. We appreciated the few close friends who continued to come, but the sign on the door of the room asked visitors to check in with the nurses before entering the room, so we had time to prepare for meeting visitors. Kristi, who became our go-between with the outside world, answered our phone calls at home. She kept us supplied with fresh laundry and took care of Shane. Dave and I didn't have to do anything but be with Brad.

Kristi received constant phone calls from our friends with offers to help and provide meals. She didn't know what to tell them and tried to politely decline, since there was already an excess of food in the refrigerator. We were overwhelmed by the outpourings of love that continued to arrive at our home in the form of meals and cards.

My mom arrived from Sacramento on Wednesday. Although she had visited us just the month before, she wanted a chance to see Brad again. She also helped Kristi with the things that needed to be done outside the hospital.

By Thursday, the time was dragging slowly. Dave left occasionally for short periods of time to check on things at work. A few times each day, I walked up and down the five flights of stairs outside Brad's room for some exercise. Often I sat next to the window and looked down on the construction site below, where workers and machines were making a parking garage. The January ground was a mess of slushy mud and patches of snow. It was mesmerizing, the little people and big machines, moving metal braces, digging holes. It was somehow comforting to watch people with a purpose. They knew what they were making, how to fit the parts together, and what the completion date should be.

Life itself doesn't fit into such a neat set of blueprints. There are no load limits to indicate maximum stress. No one knows how long it will take for any individual to finish the project of living. We didn't know how long Brad had left, or even why he was not allowed to die. Just a month before we would have taken any measure available, in fact had done so, to try and keep him alive. But now the joy was gone. He had stopped talking, eating, smiling, moving, stopped waking up. He only breathed, long, noisy breaths, in and out. They sounded tiring and unnatural.

Friday evening all of our children and their spouses gathered at the hospital. They had left the hospital Monday evening feeling deep sadness. Dave had an idea to make this a more pleasant time together.

We sat in a circle around the room and took turns telling positive memories of times with Brad. Each story led to a new memory from someone else, and soon we were all laughing and feeling the happy influence that Brad had always had on those around him. Brad gave no indication of whether he could hear the stories. I hope he did. When it was time for everyone to go home, they took with them the positive outlook that Brad had carried throughout his life.

Brad was receiving oxygen, which the doctors assured us was not life support, just a comfort measure. Still, it seemed to Dave and me that the air blowing into his nostrils might be stimulating him to continue to take breaths. On Saturday, Dr. Bowens turned the oxygen down to a lower level. Nothing changed. He still breathed, inhaling in a quick gasp, exhaling slowly through his mouth, like he was being coached to keep that rhythm.

On Sunday we skipped the hospital church service. It was just down the hall and only thirty minutes long, but we weren't leaving the room. It was Emily's second birthday, and we were sorry to miss the party she was having with the other family members. I had not been able to shop for a gift for her, but Steph from child life had taken care of it for me, choosing a toy from the stash in the clinic and even wrapping it for Emily.

Brad still breathed on and on. I wondered if he was choosing to stay alive until after Emily's birthday. The construction site was deserted, the workers home with families. Our room was quiet. I had brought Brad's CD player and some of his favorite country CD's and tried playing them as suggested by the hospital staff in case Brad was still able to hear. It might be a comfort to him. But I can listen to country music only in short doses at the best of times, so I turned it off. Silence was more comfortable.

We talked to the Sunday night nurse about Brad's condition. How long did she think it would be? Surely she had seen people die before. It turned out she had not, and it appeared that she wanted to keep that statistic intact. No one dies here, not on my shift. Most people take their kids home. Well, we weren't most people, just parents doing what we felt was the right thing for our son under the circumstances.

Chapter 37

FRIENDS TO THE END

Monday morning Dr. Bowens came by. We talked about the oxygen again, how we felt it might be keeping him alive. He looked at the gauge. It was back up again! Had the night nurse increased the oxygen level just to keep Brad alive through her shift? Dr. Bowens turned it back to the lower level, and we agreed that if things hadn't changed by afternoon he would turn it off and see what happened.

The day went on, the construction crew was back on the job, the rest of the world having a regular Monday. We sat in that little room, looking westward toward the hills above Salt Lake City, waiting for our son to die.

Dave and I talked about the similarities between birth and death. It is like running a tape forward, then playing it in reverse. A baby is waited for, anticipated, unknown. When it is born it is completely dependent and works gradually toward independence and the ability to care for itself. As death approaches a person becomes ever more dependent, until at last he requires complete care, just like a newborn. Then comes waiting, only with sadness, not excitement. Finally, the passage to a new life, as that person goes to a place no mortal can follow.

At about 3:30 p.m. Dr. Bowens returned. He kept to his agreement, and after making sure it was what we wanted, he turned off the oxygen. The response was almost immediate. Brad took shallower breaths, slower, quieter, farther apart. The doctor glanced at the heart monitor, and then turned it off before quietly walking out and closing the door. It was just the three of us, Brad, Dave, and me. His last breath was at 3:50 p.m., Monday, January 25, 1999. I looked up in the room to try and catch a glimpse of his spirit leaving as I have heard others describe, but there was nothing visible. He was gone.

Nearly two hours later, when I didn't know how I could walk out of that hospital room and leave him behind forever, there was a quiet knock at the door. Steph, Brad's close friend from child life at the clinic came in. Her presence pulled me back to reality. She talked with us for a few minutes, sharing some happy memories of Brad. We packed the rest of his belongings, hugged Steph, and went home.

The night of Brad's viewing at the funeral home was clear and extremely cold. It was an experience I thought I would rather skip, until his friends started to come. Dave had gone earlier with Curtis, who came from Venezuela for the funeral, to dress Brad for burial. As a final touch that Brad would have loved, Dave tucked into his hands his favorite hat, the one that he had confiscated from Janene that said "Bad Hair Day." The room was filled with flowers and butterfly-shaped balloons. People came by the hundreds, standing outside in the freezing temperatures to let us know that Brad had been important in their lives.

At the funeral the next day the chapel was filled to capacity. After a program that was a wonderful tribute to his life, we went to the cemetery. Many of Brad's Camp Hobe friends were there. At the graveside, most of the people stayed only long enough for Nathan to give the prayer to dedicate the grave. It was a beautiful sunny day, but the temperature still felt like January. Our family lingered a short time, then turned to go back to our cars, when we were met by a group of Brad's friends returning to the grave. Shane Lewis explained to us that, if we didn't mind, they would like to sing the Camp Hobe song for Brad. We could think of nothing Brad would have liked more.

This group of teenagers and young adults, joined by Nathan, Janene, and our Shane, held hands in a circle around Brad's coffin and sang the camp theme song. Until that moment I had been able to control my emotions. But that changed as I watched some of Brad's closest friends, who shared a deep bond of love and understanding, paying tribute to him in a way I know he would have chosen himself if it were possible. They were, in every sense, friends to the end.

CAMP HOBE SONG

We all know just why we come here.
It's the feelings that we share,
The old friends and now some new ones,
Letting each know that we care.

We are free to share our laughter,
And at times we speak with tears.
It's this place we call Camp Hobe,
That has helped us through the years.

So come on let's sing together.
Raise our voices `cause we're one.
We're the kids who make Camp Hobe
The best place beneath the sun.

Though the years may separate us,
Sending each on our own way
We can take the things we learn here
With us every single day.

So here we are today at Hobe
Joining hands and sprits too.
We will always treasure moments spent
Together---me and you.

Chapter 38

OUR TREASURE CHEST

Just as Brad earned a reward from the hospital's "Big Red Toy Chest" after difficult procedures, our family received a new treasure with each trial we endured. These experiences now fill our personal "hope chest". All were bought with a price, as were the rewards Brad received. Occasionally, I take one out and examine it. The treasures include faith that Heavenly Father is watching over us in more ways than we know; appreciation for good people, for health when we have it, for earth's beauty, and for family; the promise of an eternity of joyous experiences with those we love. We would not have chosen to fill our treasure chest in the manner it happened. But we would not now want to give up any of the precious gems it holds as a result of being stretched and tried in the Lord's way.

A few weeks after Brad died we visited the Monarch Butterfly Sanctuary in Pacific Grove, California. There we witnessed a beautiful scene that seemed to represent the vision Brad had shared with us while he was in the hospital. Through a frame of butterflies and pine trees we observed flowers, deer, and the ocean, its turquoise waves endlessly breaking on the beach. In that quiet moment we savored the memories of Brad's life and the treasures that came through our experiences with him.

Brad is never far from our hearts or thoughts. We love to watch butterflies, a physical reminder of the joy he brought into our lives. I have had glimpses into his present state. He is still learning, still worshipping Heavenly Father, and still smiling.

ON BUTTERFLY WINGS

He said, "Dad, there are butterflies filling the air,
All colors and sizes---They're everywhere!
My life's about done here, I'm tired you know.
It's so beautiful there, Dad, can I go?"

I looked at my child and the glow in his eyes;
Though my heart broke to say it, I gave this reply,
"You can go when it's time, son, I'll wait right beside you.
When you let go of my hand the angels will guide you."

His last breath expired, his young life ran out,
Then I clung to the vision he'd told me about.
And the weight in my heart I can bear now it seems,
As sorrow lifts off me on butterfly wings.

By Diane Coles

EPILOGUE

More than a year had passed since Brad's death. One morning Dave woke me up early, urgently telling me to come and look at the front lawn. He was so serious and adamant that I jumped up, still groggy and wondering what was wrong. Eggs thrown at the house? Had we been TP'd? He took me downstairs to stand in front of the plate glass window in the living room.

As soon as I looked out I was reminded what day it was: Brad's eighteenth birthday. Someone else had remembered it as well. There on the corner of the yard was a banner proclaiming, "In Honor of the Great Brad Coles. May his Memory Help Bring Butterflies into our Lives Forever." We suspected right away who might have put it up, and after calling Brad Crawford found out he was the thoughtful person that kept our sons memory alive in his heart, as we and many of his friends do.

I have heard tales of friends going to the cemetery to play games or have a picnic next to Brad's grave. Sometimes when we visit there we see unusual gifts: an open bottle of soda, a stick of gum, notes, and of course butterflies.

When I started looking through the contents of Brad's room, I found something I wish I had known about before his death. For an English class assignment during the last semester he attended school, he had written his own eulogy. Had I found it sooner it would have been read at his funeral. Since we missed that opportunity, I include it here as the way he wanted the world to remember him.

MY EULOGY, By Brad Coles

Brad Coles, he was a good kid, but not too good. Of course he made some bad mistakes but in the end he fixed what was wrong. He was a very loving boy to all his friends. He loved to hang out all night long with his friends and I saw him say "hi" to everyone as he walked down the hall.

He was very well known as I have been told. He would be happy most of the time even if he was in a bad mood. He was very funny. I could tell he liked hanging out with the girls because that is where I saw him the most. I think his saying was 'The more the merrier."

His favorite subject I do believe was English with that great teacher---What's her name?---Oh yeah, Mrs. Payne; just kidding Mrs. Beach. Man, thank goodness he is dead or he probably would be if she heard that. (This was written for an assignment in Mrs. Beach's English class.)

I think Brad's interest was cartoon drawing. He could draw almost any Disney or Warner Brothers cartoon. He also loved to snow ski and snow board. He was a great snow skier, but not so great at snow boarding. That never stopped him though from still going. I would like to think of him as a beginning snow boarder.

He was really good when it came to knee boarding though. He could do so many tricks. It was a great time watching him out on the water. But, of course you know his biggest interest: GIRLS! I'm surprised that it's not what killed him, going after so many girls. He liked working on the computer. He has his own graphics computer program. I believe the thing he did best was putting together parties for cancer kids and family members.

I didn't know a more determined person to set goals and try to reach their goals. I know he accomplished his goal to become an Eagle Scout and did it when he was only thirteen years old. His main goal in life was to work for Disney or Warner Brothers as a graphic cartoon artist and become pals with the head man or woman in charge of the company. He also wanted to finish school all the way through college. He planned to get married by the time he was twenty five and have four to five kids, two or three boys and two girls.

In Brad's family there are eight people altogether. His mom and dad, Dave and Diane Coles; his sister Alisa who is twenty three years old and is married with a one year old little girl named Katie and now is pregnant with her second child. His second oldest sister, Kristi, is twenty one years old and married with two kids, a two month old baby named Matthew and a one year old girl named Emily. His other sister Janene is twenty and just got married last summer and now is expecting her first baby. His oldest brother Nathan is eighteen and is going to school at BYU. He loved having Mrs. Beach for his English teacher in high school. Brad was next in the family. Last is his youngest brother Shane who is nine years old. Sometimes he was annoying, but he was good for playing video games with Brad.

All in all this life was good until it got worse. Now if you knew the boy like I did, you would have known that he had cancer for fourteen years. One night he started to cough and had a really hard time breathing. His parents rushed him to the hospital and were told the cancer was now in his lungs and he didn't have very many days left to live. He spent two days at the hospital and asked if he could go home and pass away in his own bed. The doctors agreed and said good bye for the last time. Brad passed away near his family at his bed side late that night.

And that is what I like to call the most amazing man that I have ever seen in my life. Even when he was sick he was smiling. He is a friend of mine that can never ever be replaced. So, good bye and farewell my friend. You will always be with us forever.

Your bud, pal, and mostly friend,
SPAM MAN JUNIOR